THE BOY FROM EL MIRAGE

A MEMOIR OF ODD BEGINNINGS, UNEXPECTED MIRACLES, AND WHY I HAVE NO IDEA HOW I WOUND UP WHERE I AM

A TRUE STORY

THOMAS HORN

DEFENDER

CRANE, MO

The Boy from El Mirage: A Memoir of Odd Beginnings, Unexpected Miracles, and Why I Have No Idea How I Wound Up Where I Am

Defender Crane, MO 65633
©2017 by Thomas Horn.
All rights reserved. Published 2017.
Printed in the United States of America.

ISBN: 978-0-9981426-9-2

A CIP catalog record of this book is available from the Library of Congress.

Cover illustration and design by Jeffrey Mardis.

All Scripture quotations from the King James Version; in cases of academic comparison, those instances are noted.

Contents

Introduction

From Womb to Tomb…and Beyond

I have no idea how I wound up where I am. In fact, sometimes I feel like the most unqualified man on earth to be out here addressing global audiences through syndicated media on television…speaking at these huge conferences where thousands of people have crowded into large auditoriums to hear me, of all people.

THOMAS HORN, in the introductory scene of SkyWatch TV's documentary, INHUMAN: The Next and Final Phase of Man Is Here, 2015

People are dreamers by nature. From childhood, we are constantly trying on different personalities or roles, shuffling through the varying facets of who we are and developing ways to nurture certain ideas and steer away from others while we settle into our identities. When circumstances require it, we find ourselves slipping out of one identity and into another to react to our surroundings, all the while taking mental notes that for most of us will last a lifetime and assist us in understanding ourselves later on when we are confronted with more important decisions than childhood usually presents. As we reach our teen years, we begin to put the pieces of life together in a way we hadn't ever before, and although most of us experience a know-everything period—that moment when adulthood maturity first takes root and is backed by an all-new level of confidence behind choices that maybe are *not* ideal—it is during this time when we start to understand who we really are through the victories we experience and the mistakes we make.

Once identity, even on a subconscious and early level, is established, our deepest and sincerest longings (the Bible refers to these as the "desires of the heart," *not to be confused with temporary desires of the flesh*) begin to call out to us like a quiet needling that pricks our cognition over and over again. Try as we might, we cannot silence the voice of these dreams, and we find ourselves repeatedly drawn to them. Many even attempt to pursue their grand vision before the timing is right, so they face disappointment and believe then that they have been shown a sign that their dream is not realistic.

But it is for those moments we have the Holy Spirit to continue prodding us.

Humans on earth live in this current, temporal reality, limited by only what one person is capable of feeling or observing. All around us, however, is a realm unseen by man: an ever-present and active spiritual domain. This is a different side of our earthly reality—far superior than anything we can comprehend in this life. Within this domain, God places His calling upon individuals to follow His lead. Unfortunately, the verses in the Bible in which Christ calls for mankind to "deny himself" (Luke 9:23), or others that similarly speak of "laying aside the old self" and "putting on the new self" (Ephesians 4:22–24), have been blasted from some pulpits for centuries suggesting that all our hopes, dreams, and desires must be vigorously muzzled in order for us to accomplish full obedience to the Lord. Understandably, this leads many to believe that everything we want or crave is "of the flesh." When this argument is raised among churchgoers, invariably some speak up and counter this with an excerpt from Psalm 37:4, reciting only that God will give us "the desires of our hearts." However, the most balanced approach to this talk of dreams and desires is to realize that all of these verses complement each other.

If Paul wrote in Galatians 2:20 that Christians have been "crucified with Christ; and it is no longer [us] who live, but Christ who lives in [us]; and the life which [we] now live in the flesh [we] live by faith in the Son of God"—and, if we read in Jeremiah 1:5 that the One who created the universe molded us to be who we are before we were ever conceived in the womb—then we arrive at a fresh perspective: The Lord *does wish* to give us the desires of our hearts, and those desires should never be silenced, primarily because *He* is the one who put them there. He played His part in creating us before our biological parents did. It just so happens that with Christ living in us, our old self was crucified with Him, therefore our desires are God-given and harmonize with His access to using us in that area of interest and ministry.

For every child born into this world, there is a *purpose*.

For every purpose that is *fulfilled*, a footprint is left behind.

These footprints can never be erased throughout the throes of history—no matter how celebrated or infamous one's role is perceived as being by others who follow. When considering the concepts behind the Butterfly Effect, meteorologists have famously hypothesized that one single flap of a seagull's wings could potentially forever alter global weather patterns from that moment forward. If a nameless, uncelebrated, and completely random seagull might have such a profound impact on this planet in the opinion of respected scientists, imagine how much more a human could be capable of, *whether or not* he or she ever reaches a level of public fame or acclaim.

Some born into this world will rise like the Davids from humble beginnings and conquer enormously intimidating giants in nothing more than field clothes and with no more than a sling and the Holy Spirit's steady aim…and everyone will talk about what those people have done for hundreds or thousands of years. Others, like Mary Magdalene, will appear as a thorn to society until the day their faith, humility, and stories of redemption inspire uncountable masses to believe in their own restoration. Still others may live their lives quietly, seemingly uneventfully, like a seagull flapping its wings over a peaceful tide, never wholeheartedly grasping the importance of its existence and how the tiniest of decisions can potentially forever alter the globe. The Davids, the Mary Magdalenes, and the seagulls *all* leave a footprint, and the world would never be the same without them.

It is easy to feel consumed by the idea that the heroes of old were always aware of their role in this temporal game of life, drawn into a masterful plan through signs and wonders. This is especially true in a time when society applauds competition and activism everywhere we turn, as if to suggest that it is only those who raise their flags of peace or beat their drums of war that contribute to humanity. It's like there is an invisible, hovering sign in the skies that reads, "Those who are not born into or for fame and greatness are unimportant." It is likewise easy, then, to adopt the notion that only "the heroes" make a difference. Such a concept not only disrespects the value of human life, but it stunts individuals from otherwise achieving God's ultimate plan for their lives because they are led to feel less important than "the heroes of old." And if each man, woman, and child is known by the Almighty God before he or she was ever formed in the womb (Jeremiah 1:5; Psalm 139:13), and if even the very quantity of hairs on each person's head is numbered (Matthew 10:30; Luke 12:7)—which suggests that God's concern for every soul on earth extends to the most finite detail—then *every* life, regardless of how many scribes or journalists reference that life later, has a purpose—and, by extension, leaves a footprint.

Let's take the story of Moses, for example, simply because it is a familiar account. As most of us know, Moses was born when the Pharaoh of Egypt had enslaved all the Hebrews, beat them mercilessly, and forced them to carry out hard labor in the sweltering sun. He then ordered that all male Hebrew babies were to be drowned, because he felt threatened by the growing population and believed that the Hebrews were becoming strong enough to wage war against him. Moses' mother, Jochebed, hid her newborn from the Egyptians for a few months, but when she realized she wouldn't be able to keep the baby hidden any longer, she made a basket, covered it in pitch, and sent him down the river. When the Pharaoh's daughter saw the child drifting by, she drew him out of the water, named him Moses, and raised him in the presence of Egyptian royalty. As an adult, Moses fled to the desert to avoid the death penalty after he killed an Egyptian soldier who was beating a Hebrew man. Arriving in Midian, Moses met and married Zipporah and became a shepherd for his father-in-law's flocks. One day in the desert while he was standing amongst the sheep, Moses saw a burning bush. The Angel of the Lord spoke to him from the bush, telling Moses to return to the people he had left behind, speak to the Pharaoh, and tell the Egyptian leader he must release the Hebrew nation from bondage. Equipped with the ability to perform supernatural feats, Moses obeyed, despite his fear. Alongside his older Hebrew brother, Aaron, the two men carried out the task God had given them. When Pharaoh refused to release the Hebrews, ten plagues from heaven inflicted misery upon the Egyptians, so, eventually, Pharaoh agreed to let the people go. Changing his mind later, Pharaoh sent his armies to track down the Hebrews. When Moses and the Hebrews leaving Egypt reached the edge of the Red Sea, Moses cried out to the Lord as Pharaoh's marching armies began to get close and closer behind them. The Lord instructed Moses to hold up his staff over the sea. The waters parted, and the Hebrews crossed through the body of water to the other side. Pharaoh's men followed the Hebrews onto the then-dry bed of the sea, but the waters crashed down upon them, drowning the Egyptians in the same way they had drowned the Hebrews' young. Once freed, the people trekked to Mt. Sinai, where the Law, as well as the Ten Commandments written by the hand of God on stone tablets, was given to the nation of Israel through Moses.

In this story, Moses is the most visible hero. He is not, however, the *only* hero.

Many are aware that Moses was to be killed just after he was born because of Pharaoh's decree to throw all male babes into the Nile. But a more overlooked part of the narrative is that Moses was never supposed to be born in the first place, as Pharaoh had instructed the midwives of the Hebrews to perform a crude type of early abortion on every male child:

> And the king of Egypt spake to the Hebrew midwives, of which the name of the one was Shiphrah, and the name of the other Puah: And he said, "When ye do the office of a midwife to the

Hebrew women, and see them upon the stools; if it be a son, then ye shall kill him: but if it be a daughter, then she shall live."

EXODUS 2:15–16

As we read along in the story, we see the hand of God upon Moses' life and the lives of the other Hebrew boys play out from the beginning:

But the midwives feared God, and did not as the king of Egypt commanded them, but saved the men children alive.... Therefore God dealt well with the midwives: and the people multiplied, and waxed very mighty.

EXODUS 2:17–20

This order to kill babies from the birthing stool was given and disobeyed long enough before the birth of Moses that the people had "multiplied" and become "mighty" by the time Jochebed of the Levites gave birth to Moses. We will never know the number of male children who were born in this interim, nor will we know how many were allowed to grow into manhood or teen years prior to the Pharaoh's next murderous rampage, but we know that, because of Shiphrah and Puah's one historic decision, a nation was able to multiply—and, at least for a time, babies were allowed to live. Not only was Moses saved from the unscrupulous murder order, but so, too, were scores of others whose personal stories, if written, would have made incredible and fascinating memoirs.

I can see the modernized title now: *Babe in the Hands of Pharaoh: The True Story of One Life Saved by Shiphrah*. One might wonder today what amazing tales of triumph and victory would have trailed such souls had they been given access to an Internet blog site. Or perhaps: *Wrath of Pharaoh, Wrath of God: Puah's Account of Obedience Toward God and*

Against Egypt. Imagine the inspiration we might gain from these women and their professions had they access to update their Facebook profiles just after this era of unspeakable tension when they made their decision—*that one historical decision that changed the course of the world*—to follow God instead of the Pharaoh. What a ministry they might have had! And here's another: *Jochebed and the Basket Baby: How One Woman's Choice to Relinquish Her Child Ultimately Led to Freedom for All of Israel.* Talk about a serious drama. A tale of woe, faithfulness, surrender, and reunion would have followed if Jochebed had been given instructions on how to build a Kindle book through Amazon. People who have children of their own almost can't fathom the heartbreak this woman would have felt the moment she placed her sweet baby boy into that pitch-and-slime-covered basket of bulrushes and sent him down the Nile River to what might have been a cruel, violent, or miserable end. Nor can they fully comprehend the joy she would have experienced when she was brought to the Pharaoh's daughter a short while later to nurse the very baby she had let go!

So many, *many* stories were never wholly shared out of just *one* biblical narrative; they were only silenced by the limited means of documentation at that time. Everyone has a story. There is no time like the present to live it to the fullest.

Certainly, had the midwives made the wrong decision and gone along with the abortion plan, or had Jochebed allowed the Egyptian soldiers to take her child, another Moses could still have been born simply because God is all powerful and could have made a way. However, that alternate story, too, likely would have involved someone who was willing to make the right decision and *be used by God* to bring it about. Someone had to make the right determination with willpower and resolve.

Everyone remembers Moses, but without Shiphrah, Puah, and Jochebed *or* others God might have chosen to use, there never would have been a Moses. The choices we make on a day-to-day basis in this life are important, no matter how old we are, what family we come from, how much money we have, how many degrees are behind our names, how many people we know, or how charismatic our personalities are. Maybe we are born to be the next David or Moses so we can free entire nations from enemies or slavery. Maybe we are born to be the next Mary Magdalene, Shiphrah, Puah, or Jochebed so we can make the right decision at the right time that sets a new standard of radical obedience to God for future generations. Maybe we are born to be the seagulls or the unspecified children of Hebrew women during Pharaoh's reign of terror, whose stories are never published but whose single wing-flap alters the patterns of the planet forever.

But one thing is for sure: We are *born to be.*

Not one of us is a mistake, and from the womb, each of us is known by God and given a purpose by Him. In this, we never need doubt. Everyone has choices. There is no time like the present to make these choices wisely, believing that when we leave this world behind, our footprints can speak of lives that thrived—from womb to tomb…and beyond.

What you are about to read is *my* story. My developing footprint. The story of Thomas Horn of Defender Publishing and SkyWatch TV. Yet, it is far more than that. I hope that each of you will be encouraged to absorb the lessons that can be drawn from these pages and apply them to your own life. This domain is positively brimming with dreamers who don't understand their value, potential, and impact. If this book changes that for even one person, if even one person arrives at the end of this book with better understanding of how the Lord might be nurturing the desires of his or her heart, then my goal will be achieved. Anyone might be a hero, but it is through believing that they will achieve.

You know, I have at least one thing in common with Moses. I, too, was never supposed to be born…

But before we arrive at that detail, let us start at the very beginning.

Before the Boy...

During the 1920s, when the United States was drinking deeply from the glass of success, Vida Kendall had want for nothing. She had been born into wealth just at the turn of the century, and she enjoyed all the luxury and comfort that promises. Her parents had the highest of hopes for her landing a handsome young husband who would complement her way of life. Throughout her childhood, she was sent to the best of schools in Oklahoma, attended church, and made appearances at many extravagant and elegant soirees that were at times attended by celebrities. By the time she reached her pre-teen years, her manner was of a perfectly decent and polite Southern belle, with her whole life ahead of her. Her plump frame was a reflection of the abundance offered her at every table gathering, as well as of her ability to enjoy life to the fullest. Scarcely was there ever a free day in her packed schedule, with all the social events that needed both careful planning and brilliant execution the likes of which she had been well trained to supervise. And when she did have a free moment, she filled it with the most elaborate embroidery, sewing, knitting, and craft projects. Everything seemed to be staged for her to only continue rising in society, a near guarantee upon her future that she would be surrounded by overflowing bank accounts and security to the very end.

But then, she met Ardis McLaughlin.

He was the polar opposite of anything Vida Kendall had ever witnessed in her hometown circles: He was rugged, unpretentious, sincere, disinterested in putting on airs, and determined.

Although polite and well-mannered, Ardis had dropped out of school around the third grade, started working before he was ten years old, and lived from day to day on the pennies he earned fulfilling the dirtiest of jobs. He had absolutely nothing to offer a young lady besides his heart and his arms. His tall, lean frame was a manifestation of his habit of skipping meals that he could not afford and working harder than the human body was designed to work. Scarcely was there ever a free day in his packed schedule, what with all the hard labor that needed to be carried out, the likes of which he had been well trained to accept since money only came through sweat and blood. When he did have a day off from work, Ardis took that time to put his hands to good use fixing things in disrepair. Everything seemed to be staged for him to only continue forward in his grimy work clothes, digging trenches during torrential downpours, and wearing blisters on his shoveling fingers until the very end.

But then, he met Vida Kendall.

She was the polar opposite of any of the scrawny girls he had met in his hard life: She was curvy, sweet, well educated, articulate, and beautiful.

It was an intense connection from the start.

Vida's friends could not figure out what she saw in a bumpkin cowboy, seventeen years older than herself, adorned in overalls and muddy boots, but she cared little for their opinion anyway. Ardis, to her, was the real deal. He may not have had the same impressive vocabulary as some of her previous callers, and his drawl may have grated on the nerves of others in her position, but every word he spoke to Vida pierced her heart with milk and honey as if they had been sent by Cupid's arrow.

Ardis, likewise, didn't care one iota that Vida's figure didn't fit the ideal that society praised. To him, she was all girl. She may have been used to a life he couldn't connect with, and her poise may have been intimidating to the likes of people below her par, but every movement she made was like a graceful fairy princess straight out of a storybook, and despite all internal warnings that he could never be what she deserved, he was crazy about her.

They simply couldn't help themselves.

Vida's parents, of course, forbade the relationship, which was understandable. Letting their daughter run off with a penniless ditch digger would be unthinkably irresponsible.

That was when the secret love letters began.

For approaching a hundred years now, those letters remained hidden, only talked about in rumor. Recently, when I sent Allie Anderson and Donna Howell (Allie is my personal secretary; Donna is my lead editor and researcher—and *both* are my daughters) to Arizona to gather some research materials regarding my childhood for this book, the letters were found and graciously given to Donna to bring back with her. She obtained a special purse for her flight back, refusing to place these precious treasures in any checked baggage, lest they be misplaced by the airlines and lost forever. During her flight, Donna clutched that huge, black purse as if her life depended on it. Even when the passengers were instructed to place their personal belongings on the floor under the seat ahead of them, Donna slipped her foot through the straps of the bag, affixing it to her ankle. After she got off the plane in Missouri, she stopped by a restaurant to get dinner—and she kept that strap looped around her elbow the entire time she was eating. Not even turbulence or car theft would rob our family of these memories now.

Nobody told me the letters had been acquired. The girls kept it a secret from me until Donna had transcribed each one into an electronic document. I noticed that she had been mysteriously busy upon her arrival back, and I hadn't received any email updates from her about her work for a few days, which, for Donna, is unusual. Nevertheless, a couple weeks back at the time of this writing, she called to say she had something special to give me. She arrived a few minutes later carrying several gallon-sized freezer bags filled with what looked like various yellow and brown envelopes. What a surprise it was when I learned that what she held in her hands was a possession more valuable to me than gold. For all I knew, since those letters had only been spoken about but never seen, they had long since been shuffled around in the family, mistaken for trash, and accidently thrown away at some point. Against all odds, those love letters had survived in my family line to this day and had been well preserved. I now keep them in my personal home office.

And it is from these old, brown, creased, and faded relics of history that we can delve into the story of Ardis and Vida even deeper...

Vida continued her life in Buffalo, Oklahoma, arranging parties and living lavishly, taking classes in English, Spanish, history, and advanced physiology, and going to "the show" on weekends. In the meantime, she poured herself into this prohibited love every single night, telling Ardis over and over in immaculate cursive penmanship, "I get so darn lonesome for you I can't hardly stand it."

In his replies, Ardis always called her by the endearing pet name "Kid," and signed each one "from Buck." His letters from Shidler, Oklahoma—they were now separated by 250 miles—were far shorter, his penmanship was at times unreadable, and his spelling was all over the place due to his stunted education. But loving he also was, despite his briefness, giving her hope through his words, "My dear girl, Kid I with [wish] you was here to night."

Each letter is innocent and chaste, as was their relationship, despite the forbidden social circumstances. One creased paper after another, many of which are difficult to read as the years have rendered Ardis' pencil strokes almost illegible, the couple gave their hearts to one another over distance and time. As one might expect, Vida wrote much about her high-society schedule and social events, and Ardis responded with updates on his latest jobs, including a few instances of injury. His short, one-paragraph letters left much to be desired in the romance department, and at one point, Vida tossed in a little tease to inspire jealousy:

> You know Neta's brother…is here on a visit now. Well, he was taking Neta to a party and they just begged me to go, too, so I went.… When the party was over, it was left up to Neta and I to walk uptown. George and this other kid Harold caught up with us. Neta walked with George (which is natural) so I walked with Harold.… Then they took me home. Had quite a bit of fun. Oh, my sweetheart, I wish you were here to go places with me and <u>take care of me</u> for I need taking care of. Don't you think so? (underline in original)

In those days, simply "walking with" another boy could mean something, such virtuous days they were. Ardis was not one to be manipulated, and his next letter made that perfectly clear. With errors removed, this was his take on Vida's game:

> Kid if you like that fellow you went with go ahead and go with him. This is the first time, and it is the last time, that I'm going to say this. What I've been doing down here is looking for work. What you've been doing is having a good time.
>   Now this is all I have to say.
>   From Buck

That's Ardis for you, and just how I remember him: straightforward and honest, and always expecting the same. It wasn't that Vida had done anything especially indiscreet—and I laugh now when I think of how innocent her gesture was compared to what today's equivalent would be—but Ardis would certainly have been one to nip it in the bud, so to speak.

When Vida received her gentle rebuke, she responded with the teary outpouring and adolescent deflections you might expect from a young girl who has discovered the hard way that her new man isn't into the playing-hard-to-get thing:

> When I got your letter this evening I just sat down and cried. Honey, I didn't think that letter would hurt you like that. Oh sweetheart I love you so. I can't stand to see you hurt like that. It wasn't my fault dear I was with that one kid going down town, I either had to walk with him or by myself, and honey if I'd have thought you cared like that, why I'd have gone by myself.... I just wrote it that way to tease you but I thought you would understand how I meant it.
>   Oh my dearest, I love you so, and then to be kept away from

you, it is nearly breaking my heart. I know we can write letters, but I hate writing letters to you. I'd a whole lot rather be with you and tell you what I want to as to write to you.

Needless to say, they worked it out. After Vida's apology, the adorable little stunt was never mentioned in another exchange. In a letter Vida wrote dated September 11, 1924, we run across this gem:

Mamma has found out a lot of things. She knows we are engaged I think. You know I wonder if some of my mail isn't stopped here at Buffalo. If I thought it was, there sure would be something stirring.
  To think dear you haven't heard from me since you left and then I felt so bad when I hadn't heard from you for six weeks. Oh my dearest it must have been awful for you. I wish you lived closer so you could come and see me if not but for one day....
  Yours forever. Vida (Mc)

She even signed it with "(Mc)" as a sweet practicing of her intended's surname. Yet, as history and these correspondences tell, the day would arrive when her mail delivery was no longer suspect. If Vida's parents hadn't approved of her intentions to marry Ardis, they had little to say about it now. On October 4, less than one month from the day Vida spoke about "Mamma" discovering their secret engagement, Ardis writes:

My Dear little wife,
  I will drop you a few lines to let you know that I got home all okay. It rained all the way home on us. We walked in the ditch. We sure had a time.

I have not gone out see what is going on because we got home the next day about noon. I told my mother and sister I was a married man, and they wish us all of the happiness in life. They said they would like to see my wife. I told them you weighed 160 pounds and was all girl....

Well Kid you know I am a poor lover to write to. You tell me all of news. I close for this time, from

Buck

"My dear little wife," he had written… This must have been just after they had eloped. I remember hearing all about that while I was growing up, how Grandma McLaughlin had given up everything in her world and thrown herself into the unknown to follow her young heart.

Despite every resistance, Vida had done it. Certainly, there were those in the family lineup who cast doubting glances, assuming that this tale of youthful romance would end in tragedy when Vida saw all she would have to surrender in order to carry out this new life she had promised herself to. By no means did this go unchallenged. After she, now married, had returned to her parents' house in Buffalo—to await the day her newlywed husband would send the glorious news that the house he had prepared for them was ready for her to be carried across the threshold—she sent several updates to Ardis telling him of the teasing at school and the reputational 180-degree turn her life had taken as a result of their little rendezvous. Everyone on her end was talking about the disgrace she had engaged in, and she even spoke of how "Mamma won't let me go to school parties or anything now."

Although we may never know exactly what discouragement Ardis was hearing on his end, we can imagine he heard it all. There must have been those filling his head with the idea that as soon as Vida settled into a life without glamour and material possessions, she would become cross, blame him for lack of effort, file for divorce, and so on. This much is clear based on the next test their relationship faced, when Ardis decided to play a little game of his own. (I do love this story. This next bit sounds just like it was taken out of a Hollywood movie script.)

Vida had written and asked what kind of house Ardis was living in. (Clearly, while together, they talked most of love and future happiness and, like any teenagers or early adults would, were too swept away by romance to fully discuss realistic expectations or even the most basic of accommodations, such as where they would live.) This was important information to her, because without it, the curtains and bedspreads she was hand-stitching in Buffalo may not match the theme of her new matrimonial dwelling when Ardis later sent for her. The colors could still be chosen in a few spots to synchronize with whatever décor he may have had. And then there was the doilies she was knitting, also. The doilies would need to coordinate…

He responded on October 30, letting her know that his plan was to take her home with him the following Thanksgiving. Then he nonchalantly dropped this bomb:

> Honey you asked me where I was living now. I am living in a tent, so you can tell where we get to live. I fixed it up so we would be warm this winter. That's why I said you won't be living too much when you're here with me. I wish you was here.

The ultimate test. I cannot imagine the blow Vida must have felt receiving this news. It was the confirmation that everyone on Vida's end had been waiting for, the moment they would all be justified in giving the "I-told-you-so" lecture. Of course, those surrounding Ardis were waiting with baited breath as well to observe how little wifey would handle it. When I first read these letters, it was at this point in the unfolding story that I was most tempted to skip ahead (the letters overlapped, as they were writing each other every day, so several were written between his letter to her and her response).

On November 3, Vida revealed her shock:

My dearest husband.…

You could have knocked me over with a feather when I read your letter and you said you were living in a tent. Honey, I don't see how on earth you can live in a tent all the time… I think it would be awful cold. Dear, can't you possibly get a house?

She went on to talk about the regular daily updates in her life, she spoke about a football game at her school the following day, and asked if Ardis planned to go down and vote in the election. It was clear, however, that she couldn't let go of her trepidation over the tent…*but* she ended her words lovingly.

I don't want to live in a tent dearest. I imagine it would be awful cold in a tent and I can't imagine how on earth you can cook. What kind of furniture would we have?… Well dearest, I must close with lots of love and kisses.

Your most loving and faithful wife, Vida.

Before Ardis had received this, Vida wrote another letter the very next day. Certainly, she hadn't accepted the notion of living in a tent, and she voiced her concerns, as well as her mother's understandably shocked reaction, for several pages. But what is most incredible is how devoted she remained. This was her closing:

> Now listen dear, won't you try your best to get a room for us to live in this winter instead of living in a tent? Sweetheart I wish you would. It would be so much better.... Well dearest I'll have to close for this time with lots of love & kisses.
> Your wife Vida.
> Remember dear, I love you more than any person on earth.

Her true colors. The real girl inside, when all the grandeur was threatened. She was going to stay with him even if it meant they would be living in a tent!

And then, the truth came from Ardis a couple days later:

> My dearest wife,
> I read your letter. I was glad to hear from you.
> Listen Kid, I already have a land of my own. I just told you about the tent to see what kind of a girl I married. Kid I knew you would stay with me through life. Honey it's easy to tell one another how much we love them, but it takes more than talk to prove it.

Well, now they were even! She had played her game, he had played his. Game, set, match. Each proved to the other throughout extreme duress and a period of miserable separation that they were in it for the long run. Vida was not at all angry about Ardis' trick, but instead sent words of great relief, respect for his position, and continual expressions of longing.

And the rest is history.

Although there were more letters in the bundle from later on when work called Ardis away intermittently through the '20s and '30s (those letters are also dripping with sincerity and love), the last of this string ended on November 20, after they exchanged a discussion of Ardis' plans to come for Vida on Thanksgiving. True to his word, he brought her home with him to live on his land, and within a couple of years, my uncle Jack was born. Following that, my mother, Sally, was brought into the world.

At the beginning of their marriage, Ardis worked for the city on the railroads. Life trekked forward for the two lovebirds who only ever fell deeper into adoration for each other as time went on. This devotion would prove to be essential, considering the turn the country was about to take…

In late 1929, the Wall Street stock market crash turned the nation on its head with instantaneous and devastating debt. Almost everyone was affected. Many lost their homes and every material possession, and huddled together on the outskirts of the cities in dirt-floor huts built from scrap and debris within the "Hooverville shanty towns" (thus named after the victims of the market crash, who placed the blame on President Herbert Hoover). Only a little over three years later, in 1933, the "Dust Bowl" began, adding another layer of disaster to the already dire circumstances. Twenty-five thousand square miles of farmland primarily in Texas, Oklahoma, New Mexico, Kansas, and Colorado were swallowed by thick, monstrous clouds of dust in one of the longest and most devastating droughts of American history, which did not end until the following year. Dry-land farming methods had not been adequately applied, and wind erosion wrought havoc upon agricultural areas like nothing our country had ever seen before or would ever see again. Layers upon layers of the blackest dust covered what once had been the glorious greenery of the great USA. This decade would then be referred to as the "Dirty Thirties"—in an ironic and tragic contrast to its predecessor, the "Roaring Twenties."

With the harvest fields destroyed, as well as farming equipment and sometimes even homes (after the more aggressive of these storms, many had to be torn down), farmers also became travelers, with tens of thousands of families uprooting their lives to look for a fresh start elsewhere, most often to California. (By 1935, over five hundred thousand American farm civilians had become homeless.) Sadly, they discovered that the economic downfall of the nation left little for them to turn to in the cities.

Many cultural issues arose during this time that completely destroyed the lives and legacies that had been built over generations. Men, women, and children packed only their most precious heirlooms and, with little more than the clothing on their back, headed out in "jalopies" (old, worn-out cars) carrying basic survival materials strapped to the vehicles with rope wrapped around the exterior from every angle. Most had nowhere to go as they drove aimlessly toward the unknown to look for work. Staying with relatives was often out of the question, since entire extended families—and their farmlands—had suffered the same fate. Hard-working farmhands were suddenly aplenty, surviving farms had more inquiries for work than they could accommodate, and many seeking work were sent away from the cities as well, as urban areas were already inundated with the homeless and unemployed, such as those who huddled in Hoovervilles.

Some Dust Bowl migrants suffered from dust pneumonia. Others suffered from malnutrition, as food was a scarce commodity.

And yet, the roads were not traveled upon solely by displaced farming families. Lawyers, professors, small business owners, and lay workers of every variety were all just as willing to put their shoulders to the plow for a hot meal or a nickel, some of whom had dapper clothing still in their suit-cases from their romps at the jazz clubs a few years prior, should they meet someone who valued appearance at a hire. The shattering one-two punch upon the economy afflicted both rural and urban areas. Those who lived in comfy homes and whose businesses were still surviving met frequent interruption in their daily duties by men who promised *they* were the best and most honest workers available. Competition was intense.

Around this rough time, Ardis took various jobs as a farmhand for Vida's parents' farm. (It is touching to know that even though the Ken-dalls didn't initially accept the union of Vida's choice, they never aban-doned the young couple in their time of need.) Recently, we were able to sit down with a recorder and interview my sister, Vidabell (named after Vida McLaughlin), whose memory is as reliable as they come. As she remembers:

> The Kendalls were always able to keep the farm through the Depression, because they always had money, and they came from money. Both of them. It was [Ardis and Vida] McLaughlin that lost all their money, because [Ardis] was working for the railroad at the time and they had all their money tied up in two banks. They lost their money when the banks crashed....
>
> A couple times, Grandpa Kendall would have [Ardis] work for him. The crops [that Ardis tended] were so good, and they were worth so much money, that Mom [my mother, Sally] said they were paid several thousand, which was a lot back then....

The money Ardis earned from the Kendall farm was used in part to purchase a vehicle to further his and Vida's ability to travel. From potato and cotton fields to lemon and orange groves to pea and berry farms and so many others, the automobiles—the McLaughlins' as well as the other Dust-Bowl migrants'—clunked and sputtered from field to field, producing people of all ages willing to pick anything, to plow anything, to till anything, to do the dirtiest of jobs for the smallest pay, and when the harvest was complete, the engines crackled to life once more as the entourage moved on to the next agricultural shrine. Between stops, anything found on the side of the road was a treasure worth pulling over to collect. A sunburnt potted plant that had fallen from someone else's wares wagon could be nursed back to health and sold for a penny at the next town, providing the traveler had a green thumb and extra water. A box of plates that had fallen and shattered into thousands of pieces was a beautiful mosaic just waiting to be canvassed. A random sheet of metal was a new roof at the next shack. An old board could hold anything together. There was a use for everything; nothing went to waste. With enough creativity, a penny or nickel could be earned with every piece of abandoned trash; with enough resourcefulness, any item could be turned into a mobile home reparation.

At times, familiar faces were spotted as the migrants frequented the fields, and people chose to travel together from harvest to harvest, creating a kind of spontaneous mobile community. After a hard day's work, it wasn't uncommon that the migrants would gather under the shade of someone's makeshift shelter to sing songs, dance, tell stories, and give updates about nearby work opportunities, *despite* the ever-present race to arrive at the next assignment while there were still plants to pick from. The sudden, national eviction of people from all backgrounds did cause strife many times, as men and women were forced to keep the peace within social circles they would have never mingled in before. However, the sudden, national eviction of people from all backgrounds was the very thing that gave them *everything* in common now, as they were all in the game of survival together. Who they once were and what they once did stopped mattering when one amidst them started to cough or lose another pound.

Recently for my birthday, my daughter Althia surprised me with the most amazing gift—a framed *Phoenix Gazette* feature article dated May 7, 1937, titled "New Generation of American Pioneers Treks Westward, Fleeing 'Dust Bowl' And Seeking New Place to Make Homes." In the picture atop the heading stands Ardis and Vida posing in front of their tent with their "jalopie," missing a headlight, on the right.

The *Gazette* was one of Arizona's top newspapers in the 1930s, and the story was an interview between a reporter and my grandparents, mother, cousins, and numerous other families who were parked alongside the road seeking shelter for their caravan under the trees, having been forced from their Oklahoma farms to pick fruit for survival. One of the original editions of the newspaper article had been in my grandfather's possession since it was originally published, kept in a small wooden box near his recliner while I was growing up, then inherited by me on his passing. I had cherished that clipping as well as the other items in the little chest—war stamps from World War II; a small, screwdriver-like tool; old work permits; and so on—until those heirlooms burned in my home in 2011. Thankfully, I had always remembered the date on which the original story had been published, because on the reverse side of the feature about Grandpa and Grandma was the historic report, "Zeppelin Explodes," all about the German passenger airship Hindenburg that had caught fire the day before, May 6, 1937, killing thirty-six people when it blew up while attempting to dock with its mooring mast at Naval Air Station Lakehurst in Manchester Township, New Jersey.

Before news had spread around the world about the Hindenburg, the top story the *Gazette* reporter had been assigned involved my family's Great Depression survivors trudging through Arizona on their way to the Promised Land—sunny California, with its sprawling fruit orchards and miles of row crops where work was waiting for desperate manual laborers.

The article reads:

Driven from farm homes in the "dust bowl" states of Oklahoma, Arkansas, Texas, and Kansas, hundreds of small scale farmers are trekking westward, seeking new homes. They are finding the hardships almost as desperate as those of the pioneers. They remained in home states until resources were exhausted, then loaded up ramshackle automobiles and started aimlessly westward, looking for work or new farms. Most of them work in the fields. Right now strawberry picking occupies a large number.

Here are pictures taken in the Salt River Valley, showing some of the drought "refugees." At the left are Mr. and Mrs. McLaughlin, who are camped near Glendale. They both work in the berry fields. Before Oklahoma became part of the "dust bowl" they were making a "good living" on a farm. Huge, bollowing [sic] dust clouds, which they describe vividly, swept the grain fields time after time, ruining crops.

"We couldn't even raise enough grain for seed toward the last," McLaughlin said. "Finally, we had to leave."

The old model car, the tent, and a few other necessities are all the McLaughlins salvaged when they left. They have two children. Second from the left is a typical low-rent tourist camp near Phoenix. Many "dust-bowlers" stop at these camps, halting long enough to earn money and continue westward....

Later, in a different article, but on the same page of this newspaper, we read another bit about the report on Grandpa:

For many years Mr. and Mrs. McLaughlin were wheat farmers in Oklahoma. Then came the dust storms.

"We tried time and again to raise crops, but the dust storms and droughts came along and caused us to lose everything. We're looking for a new home now."

The McLaughlins have two children. They have been picking strawberries for a living. (*The Phoenix Gazette*, Phoenix, Arizona, Friday, May 7, 1937)

As ironic as it may seem, by the mid 1930s, Ardis and Vida McLaughlin, my grandparents, were, as fate would land them, *living in a tent*. I don't believe Grandpa Ardis ever would have believed that was a possibility back when he wrote his letter to Vida promising her a "fixed-up" and warm tent for their first winter together.

Yet, the legacy left behind through Ardis and Vida's craft and cunning has inspired the generations that followed. This is how it began, as related by Vidabell:

They went berry picking and when they got the first trailer tents, they cooked over the campfire for many years. Mom [Sally] was a teen when they got their first trailer house. It was real small, but it had an icebox and a stove. Then, by the time she was seventeen, they got a bigger trailer house, but they still continued to work in the field.

Grandma Vida would make a stop in each town at the local thrift shops and specifically seek out any clothing or fabric that had been torn or stained, take them back to her trailer, and fix them up, then sit by her open window and sell them to the fieldworkers while Ardis was out picking. We still have photographs of Grandma standing at the window of her makeshift store. Vidabell recalls:

> They saved enough money doing that [berry picking], and then the doctor told [Vida] her arthritis was so bad she had to come here to Arizona. [Her arthritis likely set in at a younger age than it would have as a result of her constant needlework.] That's when they became the first settlers in El Mirage. They put up a little store there—a trailer store they would take to the fields— but also, [Ardis] got busy building cabins.

These cabins are a cherished memory. Grandpa Ardis would take all kinds of abandoned plywood and sheet metal scraps out of his hoarded arsenal and nail them together, building walls that at first might appear similar to the tip-over Hooverville shanty huts. Then, he reinforced the walls from top to bottom with rope and yards of chicken wire. Once it was considered sturdy enough to be a starting point, he encrusted the structure with layer upon layer of concrete as he could afford to buy it. As a finishing touch, he plastered the walls inside and out with a stucco-style rough finish to hide the clunky center. The flooring was also a poured-and-swept concrete finish. By the time Ardis was finished, each cabin appeared to have been built by a professional builder.

Because the Dust Bowl migrants had become a kind of family of their own, bonding at each stop, Grandpa saw a lucrative opportunity and built the first campsite in El Mirage. Prior to their arrival there, El Mirage was far less than any real settlement. There really weren't any stores or towns, and the landscape was primarily made of endless scenes of desert land. The location was an ideal midpoint between farms, however, and travelers would pull in and pay a fee to stay in a cabin between jobs to stretch out their legs after being cooped up in their tiny, worn-out cars. Just like the impromptu campsites that rose up at the edge of the fields, the workers would congregate outside the cabins and share stories, play dilapidated instruments, talk about Scripture, and relate to one another's difficulties.

Before long, Grandpa had enough money to put in water lines and drain pipes for the RVs, gaining the additional business of those passing through in larger vehicles. Still other additions to the campsite such as shower rooms and laundry rooms were quickly funded, bringing huge relief to those on the road who hadn't experienced the luxury of a shower or clean clothing in well over a month. Vida maintained her sales as well. My sister Vidabell shares:

> Grandma had a store in their house and the renters and farmers and ranchers and cowboys would come there and buy a new set of clothes or socks or whatever. Once a month they'd come in for new clothes, and they would wear those clothes all month long while working. Then they'd come in once a month and buy more. I would hate to be their girlfriend or wife or whatever. [Everyone in the background of the recording laughs at this sentiment.]

Wherever and whenever a penny could be earned, Grandpa Ardis was on top of it, and he and his wife had the *only* settlement in that area, so competition of any kind was scarce. If a passerby arrived without a penny to his or her name, Ardis and Vida were more than happy to extend their campsite and all of its accommodations at no cost. After all, they knew what it was like to go hungry. In fact, it was quite a regular practice that Grandma would cook up a batch of vittles or bread or whatever ingredients she could get her hands on and share them with everyone at the site. She also mothered the residents, tending to any needs that arose, including caring for those who were sick or or watching someone's children for an afternoon. If someone was able to afford to pay a fee for any service, the payment was graciously accepted, but even those who couldn't pay were generously fed, housed, and nurtured. This placed Grandma and Grandpa in the unique position of not only securing the exclusive business of everyone who passed through, but also of gaining everyone's respect and trust. In addition, their upstanding and relief-work style approach to the business brought a whole new level of appreciation of the true meaning behind Matthew 25:35–40:

> For I was an hungred, and ye gave me meat: I was thirsty, and ye gave me drink: I was a stranger, and ye took me in: Naked, and ye clothed me: I was sick, and ye visited me: I was in prison, and ye came unto me. Then shall the righteous answer him, saying, Lord, when saw we thee an hungred, and fed thee? or thirsty, and gave thee drink? When saw we thee a stranger, and took thee in? or naked, and clothed thee? Or when saw we thee sick, or in prison, and came unto thee? And the King shall answer and say unto them, Verily I say unto you, Inasmuch as ye have

done it unto one of the least of these my brethren, ye have done
it unto me.

As time went on, this camp gained enough attention that El Mirage
began to draw other settlers to the area. It's likely that the land would
have eventually been developed merely because of the population of
nearby cities such as Phoenix. However, it's no secret that El Mirage
grew how and when it did as a result of my grandparents' hard work and
brilliance. Their camp, initially built in the Dirty Thirties, stood until El
Mirage officially became a town in 1959. That year, all local businesses
were established as official and listed in the commerce registry books.

A sign outside their campsite pointed all travelers to "Mac's Trading
Post," now a certified, central, and recognized commerce in that area.
During the entire Depression (and for years afterward), anyone need-
ing a place to rest had more than that at little to no cost. Any friend-
less and desperate man or woman requiring assistance found that in my
grandparents' care, and as the economic travesty finally began to ebb
and travelers dwindled, the camp took on a new purpose. From that day
until the year Grandma died, it was the hub of our family. The land and
housing was all owned outright, so cousins, aunts, uncles, and occasionally close friends to the family always had a home to turn to and a cabin
to hang their hats in when they needed one.

The cleverness of Grandma and Grandpa McLaughlin not only
bought them out of starvation and ministered to countless needy per-
sons, but my family was able to stick together in a modest circle of land
equipped with laundry rooms and shower houses during a time when
these luxuries were beyond what any one of my family members could
have afforded. This also better equipped my relatives to save money over
the years and buy their own land later on when the state of Arizona

evoked the power of eminent domain in the interest of building a water tower. Arizona granted the McLaughlins the rights to own their land until death. Grandma outlived Grandpa, and sadly, after she passed on to be with our Lord in heaven in the 1980s, the remaining family tenants were evicted and given a small sum by the state to relocate.

Many books, movies, and television programs depict the Dust Bowl and Great Depression as a time when Americans were falling like flies, starving to death in broken-down automobiles on the side of the road, and falling to their knees to tearfully beg for even the smallest crust of bread to bring back to their busload of barefoot children. Allthough *there is truth* to that depiction on a case-by-case basis, it's not fair to consider that a complete representation of all who were affected during this era.

A large number of families did, in fact, survive the Dirty Thirties with hopefulness and faith in the Christian God, relying on prayer, growing close to one another, and eventually crawling out of horrific debt with all their children still alive and fed. And for just as many heartbreaking memories and statistics that can be listed about the Great Depression and the Dust Bowl, a list of incredible developments counteracts. Not only did these difficult times draw people closer to God, family, and others, lifestyle ethics were established for generations to come—generations of people who did not fear hard and laborious work, did not waste even the smallest of material possessions, did not spend money recklessly, and did not take for granted the wisdom that needed to be applied toward making decisions that altered the government and its leaders and laws.

However…

It is for good reason that we, as a nation, have *needed* to focus upon the worst of these Great Depression and Dust Bowl accounts in order to bring to light what might potentially happen should history repeat itself. It is through a collective compassion that we weep for the lives that were destroyed, the fathers who died in a fit of dust coughs, the dapper businessmen who never again rose above the economic fall, the wives and mothers who stood in line for hours every day to bring pitiable rations back to their Hooverville shacks, and all the others whose woes the world has never documented. Without these images flickering in our minds like a silent film refusing to fade in the folds of modern history, we would repeat a similar folly.

And without testimonies of fortitude and legacies such as that built by my grandparents, I can't see how we, the people, would have survived the trials. Grandpa McLaughlin may never have joined violent protestations or waved his stars-and-stripes flags in front of rallies, but he was absolutely a patriot by the truest definition of the word.

When I was a little boy there at the campsite while Grandpa McLaughlin whittled away relentlessly on a piece of tree limb (during the times when he wasn't challenging his rooster to a fight!), I'd ask him the deepest questions about life, meaning, God, the world, humanity's place in it, and the afterlife, among other subjects, including those about survival. I spent countless hours as a young man, and later as a young preacher, sitting with Grandma in their simple home or with Grandpa outside by the wood pile. I was listening and learning, absorbing a deep philosophy of life that had been honed in the fires of the deepest and longest-lasting economic downturn in the history of the Western industrialized world, itself followed by another World War, which also refined and defined everything they believed and practiced. My impressionable young soul absorbed their stories and life lessons regarding endurance, independence, honesty, hard work, faith, thankfulness, and kind-heartedness—all of which became the bedrock of my philosophical worldview. Short on cash and necessarily high in faith, they became perfect role models for me and my generation concerning the things in life that should really matter and be cherished. My grandparents have been gone now for many years, and with them went most of what I see as one of the greatest generations. And when by contrast I consider what people value today, I worry.

Perhaps now you can understand why I had to start at the very beginning, to the lives lived before my own, prior to telling you about what happened once I was brought into the world. The lessons learned from people ahead of me paved the way for the values I held dear from birth and forward. There would be no way to emphasize who I am at the core and what I have become—my footprint in the making—had I not paused long enough to respect the deeply rooted principles instilled within me at my earliest age. What my grandfather and grandmother built with their sweat, blood, and tears was not only a ministry for those in need and a pinnacle operation for the settling of what is now a thriving city in the United States, it was also the unwritten but formally rehearsed tenets of faith set in place by an unknown but patriotic country farmhand and his humble seamstress wife.

I'd like to think that America can once more be a nation of God-fearing winners, of rugged individualism and pioneering determination. I pray that the book you now hold in your hands is a first small step in this direction and a reminder for many of what once made our country the envy of the world. I choose to believe that our nation can once again honor and commit to God, glory, and greatness.

To the McLaughlins who have gone to be with the Lord, I would like to say: Thank you, Grandma and Grandpa, for your contribution to our country, for your values, and for your commitment to God and family. Your story is one I think of frequently, and when I am faced with what appear to be obstacles insurmountable, I continue to repeat to myself, "If Grandma and Grandpa did it, *I* can do it." In every business I have ever developed, including those I am operating now, I have faced challenging moments in the beginning wherein I always look back to the influence you had upon my youth and think, "If Grandma and Grandpa built it, *I* can build it." My story would be a different one if it hadn't been for what you brought to the world.

To the reader of this book, I would like to say: If I can do it, *you* can do it.

Dream big. To the Creator of the universe, there are no such things as obstacles insurmountable.

The Boy Who Wouldn't Live...Twice

Sally Horn was informed she "wasn't built" to have children. The professionals of the medical world had told her that she should never even consider having kids, lest she risk the life of both herself and her baby.

The baby could die, they said.

She could die...they said.

Despite the advice of her doctors, and perhaps due to the limited family-planning methods in existence at the time, Mom became pregnant at least six times in a short period of years. That number may have been even greater.

My older brother, Amil, was the first born to my parents, Clarence and Sally. Mom miscarried her next baby. My sister, Vidabell, came next, and her birth was followed by another miscarriage. With each pregnancy, there were high risks and major complications, and the already-narrow window to reproduce was ever closing. The threat of perishing during childbirth was, according to Mom's doctors, a real one that demanded to be taken seriously. Further, *if* she were to carry another baby all the way to full term, and *if* both she and the child were both to live, her womb likely was not hospitable enough to produce a "normal" child anyway.

When Mom discovered she was pregnant for a fourth time, she sought the advice of the medical world.

"I would suggest we abort," her doctor said, "and I would strongly recommend you consider an immediate hysterectomy."

Abort? Bring death to the child in the womb? But that wasn't what she was asking. She was going to the doctor for advice on how to keep *the baby, not* kill *it!*

But, the doctor said, it would be for the best. Sally had little chance of surviving the pregnancy this time around, and in the opinion of the professional, the baby was as good as gone already. She just wasn't meant to have children.

But…abort? In a frightened, kill-it-or-die ultimatum?

But, the doctor said, it had to be done. Sally didn't want to die during childbirth and leave her two children without a mother, did she? Did she want to go through the experience of carrying a life inside her, experiencing its movement, and then feeling her heart crush under the weight of another nearly guaranteed miscarriage? Assuming the baby could ever be born at all, did she want to take the chance she might be bringing a dysfunctional person into this world to face the lonely realities of brain damage or disfigurement?

Did she?…

No, "Sally" didn't want those things.

However, "Sally" wouldn't make a decision that should be the prerogative of God...

When my mother was a little girl, she had grown up never fearing hard work. When the Great Depression and Dust Bowl eras had struck the nation, she was carted from town to town in Grandma and Grandpa's car, where they would settle for the night in a tent—a tent they were incredibly thankful to have, since many Depression and Dust Bowl victims huddled under the trees for rest, subject to whatever dangers the weather and nature brought upon them. (Treats for her were a rare thing indeed, and at one point someone gave her an ice cream bar. She stashed it under her pillow to "save it for later when she could truly enjoy it," and when she discovered the nature of the elusive delicacy called "ice cream," and saw the soppy mess she was left with, she cried for hours.)

She assisted in the berry picking that was the family livelihood, helped scout for whatever "trash" items might be around for her mother and father to use for repair or resale, and, before long, she had undergone training to be just as valuable to the working household as anyone else. Vida, a talented seamstress, passed down to Mom ages of hand-stitching knowledge that today is an all but lost art, and throughout her time on the road, Mom learned to take any piece of clothing—no matter how small—and coordinate it to match in a patchwork that would become someone's purchased treasure. Clothing that was wrecked from every angle still had recycling potential as a quilt, a shirt, a dress, or anything else Mom's creative mind could concoct. (This precious characteristic stayed with her until the day that she, just like her mother, could no longer hand-stitch as a result of arthritis. When my children were little, they were never deprived of the most colorful, imaginative, and unique outfits that would arrive in a box annually. Although we still had to occasionally purchase new clothing for them when they needed something seasonal, my oldest was almost married by the time she had to shop for clothes on a regular basis, thanks to Mom's creativity with a needle and thread. It was the same story for all her grandkids.)

Grandma and Grandpa obtained their first trailer home—and thereby a legitimate roof over their heads—when Mom was in her early teen years. She was seventeen when they upgraded to a larger trailer house with an icebox and a stove, and it was an enormous relief that they were now able to cook indoors instead of over the improvised campfires that they had utilized since around her birth. Mom was taught to can, jar, and preserve foods—and, just like with her sewing, that skill followed her well beyond poverty. (I have never—*never in my life*—had pickles like Mom made. They didn't have that store-bought, vinegary taste to them, and it was easy to eat a whole jar in one sitting. Though the shipping was expensive, she always sent pickles along with each box of clothing, and my children, my wife, and I would fight over them to the last jar.)

Shortly thereafter, Vida McLaughlin was informed that Arizona would be the land of relief for her arthritis due to the dry heat. This brought Mom into the development of the campsite Grandpa built in El Mirage. However and whenever she was needed, Mom helped the McLaughlins in all the duties required for upkeep. Travelers stopping at the settlement had many needs, and she saw to them alongside her mother while the boys, my uncle Jack and Grandpa Ardis, would go picking or build another cabin. When she wasn't by her mother's side, feeding starving campers or tailoring a custom garment or quilt, she never hesitated to join the men in the dirty work.

Times were desperate, and Mom was no slacker.

Toys, games, recreational activities, and "play time" were nearly unheard of in her youth, and her personal belongings were scarce. Anything that didn't have the highest level of sentimental value could be reused, sold, or traded, and it often was. At least one item, however, hung around their camp that Ardis, Vida, Jack, and Mom refused to part with.

The King James Bible was given the utmost respect.

As was God.

Bible studies were a part of their daily regimen. A person could survive without just about everything else, but God was the greater "meat" for the soul, and this life is but temporary. Their "daily bread" was never a concern, because just as their bellies rumbled, God would provide a means for them to eat, just as He did for the "birds of heaven" that did not sow, reap, or gather in barns (Matthew 6:26; Luke 12:24). Clothing was a non-issue in light of their faith, because God would provide a wardrobe, just as He did the "lilies of the field" that did not spin their own cloth—but "even Solomon in all his glory" was not dressed as beautifully as they (Matthew 6:28; Luke 12:27). What worries did they have, despite any hardship, when they knew all along that God would hand over to them the things they needed? Christ, Himself, acknowledged that not even a "cubit" would be added to the length of one's life through worries of this nature (Matthew 6:27; Luke 12:25). Even the Great Depression and Dust Bowl held no power over the children of God who believed in earnest that they could—and would—thrive against all odds.

God was everywhere and in everything. Not a single hour of any given day went by that the recognition for provisions wasn't given to Him, to whom it was due. From Genesis to Revelation, Mom was given an invaluable biblical education regarding this life and how to prepare for the next. Well before Mom married, she had already been given the

lifelong skillsets for being the greatest mother anyone could ask for…
and during each moment of that life, she met challenges that would
send a spiritually weak person into a frenzy.

Mom was a lot of things, but more than anything else, she was *strong*.
A woman of *unshakable faith*.

When she was advised to abort me, told that she likely wouldn't
survive the pregnancy, and informed that I would probably perish in a
miscarriage—or be born deformed, damaged, or dysfunctional—Mom
knew that if her "daily bread" had to be left in the hands of God, the
baby would have to be left there, too. If, as the doctor had said, there
truly was a risk that she would die during childbirth or that I would be
born abnormal, she knew the One to look to regarding provisions.

But she would not abort the baby.

During Mom's pregnancy, she definitely faced more than a few scary
moments, but when I was out on the other side and our new family phy-
sician, Dr. Shackleford (who did not promote the same agenda of abortion as had the previous doctor), slapped my backside, I cried a normal,
healthy wail like any other bouncing baby boy with all the right parts in
all the right places. Mom survived delivery, recovered well, and thanked
God that He had given her the strength to trust in His provision, again.

This was my first—of many, mind you—trials in which I placed
my mother. Some are rather humorous. In a letter from my mother
to Grandma and Grandpa McLaughlin (saved in the midst of the
McLaughlin love letters and written while the McLaughlins were away
in California), we read that within my first years, I was already putting
in my two cents where it didn't belong: "The way [Amil] and Vidabell
fight anymore. I kind of dread it. Of course Joe usually gets right in the
middle of it." (Although my birth name was Thomas, I was nicknamed

"Joe" from the start, and to this day, that is how I'm referred to when visiting my family.)

Around this time, while we were living at "Mac's Trading Post" in El Mirage, development of the land around us had begun, and four or five times per day, jet planes flew close overhead to land at a nearby port. Although I don't remember it, Mom had written about how these jets would rattle the whole house.

Mom cooked a lot of beans, mashed potatoes, and salads, and every meal was made "from scratch" (as most were back then). When she wasn't mothering, according to her letters, she was handling the business of Mac's Trading Post, making sure that all the tenants were paid up on rent, seeing that all the help received their checks on time, watering the trees and flowers, and cleaning out the camp laundry rooms and "wash-houses" (showers). She busied herself not only with all the household chores a woman was expected to do—keeping us kids from fighting, washing our clothes against a metal scrubbing board and stringing them up to dry on a clothesline, cutting our hair, cooking, sweeping, mopping, ironing, mending clothes, and tending to Dad's sunburns after he spent long days at work—but also with finding something, *always something*, for her hands to do. Potty-training me evidently wasn't always a picnic, either, as she stated: "I've got Joe on the pot, and he's mad. He went in his pants again and got spanked, and he's still mad about it."

I kept Mom busy in those early days, for sure. But there were also many endearing moments. She exposed as much when she wrote: "[Joe] sure does get around, and says anything. He sees a bug, and he'll say, 'Bug bite you Mammie,' and repeats everything the other kids says. He really tries to show off for me. I get tickled at him. He's always trying something new, and whatever the others try, he tries it, too."

I was also prone to accidents. I had a rather aggressive and reckless approach to life, even from the beginning. In a letter dated June 14, 1959, when the McLaughlins were again away (this time in Oregon), Mom wrote, "Joe burned a little place on his upper lip. It's pretty sore. You should have heard him singing 'Along Came Jones.'"

When Donna and Allie, my daughters, asked my sister Vidabell about the time I built a "speed ramp" to jump off of with the neighborhood kid's bike—after which followed a full body-scraping—she answered, "Yeah, he was always pulling off stuff like that. He was always prone to accidents and stuff because he was always building things and they just—Well, they just wouldn't work out." This was a hilarious moment; everyone listening to Vidabell in the recording laughed out loud and clapped. "You know, both boys were kinda like that. Amil was always jumpin' off the woodpiles at Grandma's and getting nails in him. And *Joe* would do that, too."

Poor Mom. Always pulling out nails and "fixin'" my boo-boos.

But the greatest accident in my life occurred when I was four years old.

I had a young friend who lived just across the street from the campsite. My sister remembers that the boy was on the other side of the road waiting for me. My intended visit was not one that Mom had sanctioned. I was never allowed to just wander around outside the camp or play in the street. However, I had a mind of my own, and there were certainly times when I pushed against the boundaries when Mom had her head turned toward her innumerable responsibilities.

Vidabell relates:

Across the road a friend of your dad's lived, and I was friends with the girls and he was friends with the boy. There really weren't a lot of cars that went by in those days, you know, back when we were living on Grandpa's camp.... And Joe ran over to see his little friend, and this car was going over the speed limit by quite a bit, and that's how that happened.

As I had raced across the street, upon contact with the speeding vehicle, I was thrown under it. A section of the running exhaust pipe was embedded in my skull, dragging me by the head down a sizable chunk of the road until the car came to a stop. I was rushed to the hospital, where it was revealed that my brain was exposed in several areas. My mother received grievous news: There was no feasible reason to believe I was going to live.

Again.

A view of the street where I was run over by a car. The friend I was running to meet lived in the house on the right.

Alternate view of the accident site. The fence delineates the side property line of Mac's Trading Post while it existed. We lived immediately behind that line, and there was no fence keeping me in at the time.

I will never know why this was the care I was given at the time, but the medical staff members who patched me up that day clearly had no idea of what they were doing, or they didn't believe my chances of living were high enough to give me the post-accident follow-up care that surviving my injuries would require. As the physicians and nurses stitched my head back together, they left rocks and dirt in my brain where the exhaust pipe had split open my head. Within days, infection began to spread in and around the area, greatly decreasing my chances of survival.

My family was heartbroken.

This was the second time that "professionals" had told my mother I was as good as gone already.

One day, Dr. Shackleford, the doctor who had delivered me, visited me in the hospital. I was near death, and he could tell that the minute he set eyes on me. At first, he played the role of visitor only, but as soon as he was alone with me and Dad, he crept up to the head of my bed, peeled the bandages back, and saw the remnants of dirt left over from the accident. Dad later explained to me Dr. Shackleford's reaction.

"Clarence, if you leave this kid in here, he's gonna die. That's a guarantee. If you get him outta here and take him to my practice, he may still die, but he has a much better chance there."

It was all Dad needed to hear.

Dad was a well-respected cop in El Mirage at that time when he wasn't working out in the sun on campsite maintenance, and most everyone at the hospital knew him. Laws of patient release were different then, so Dad simply walked up to the nurse's station, informed them that he was taking his son, and then carried me out. He immediately took me to Dr. Shackleford's home, where he cut out all of the stitches the hospital physicians had sewn, and reopened the wound, carefully picking the debris from my brain and eradicating the dirt. Once he stitched my wound back together, I remained under his constant supervision.

Lo and behold, just a few days later, my color started coming back, and the previous swelling began to decrease. Nobody is really sure to this day how I survived that horrific accident. Despite the infection, my head injuries were so significant that I should have died before I ever got to the hospital. (The hand of God, perhaps? I like to think so. Credit where credit is due, or so Mom taught me.)

I was certainly the boy who wasn't supposed to live, by all human and finite prediction.

Physically, I mended better than anyone could have hoped. I have a hefty scar on my head to this day from where it came into contact with the exhaust pipe. The damage to my brain was permanent in only one very specific way, which happens to be a miracle in itself: I lost my long-term memory. I do not remember much of my childhood with the same kind of "visual" flashbacks many people can recall like a photo or video in the archive files of the mind. But, because my family was always close enough to laugh over the best memories, I have some truths tucked into the folds of my memory simply as a result of repetitious storytelling. If I observe an event in life and refer to it now and again from that moment forward, the memory sticks, but only because it is continuously reintroduced to the short-term memory. I do remember much of my adult life, but the earliest years are almost completely gone, except for just a few precious thoughts, like Grandpa McLaughlin whittling away by his woodpile at the campsite. This is one of the reasons why, in order to write this book, I had to have my daughters Allie and Donna travel to Arizona and speak with relatives as well as dig up the solid facts from the *Phoenix Gazette* about my grandparents.

In truth, this memory damage was a small trade-off for my life. To think of the damage that accident *could have* caused for me...

I was an exceptionally lucky little boy.

This accident was by far the worst I have ever been involved in, but due to my tendency to throw caution to the wind and leap in the line of danger for a thrill in my youth, I had several other close calls. It appears, though, that a divine calling upon my life was present from the beginning, because just as soon as I had completely recovered from being run over by a car and life had returned to normal, my recreational habits began to emulate interesting qualities.

Like many young, Tom-Sawyer types, I loved to catch lizards, toads, bugs, and any other creatures I could get my hands on. There were some things I knew not to touch, like scorpions (especially the neon-colored babies, who were the most venomous), but I was always catching something. What I did with these creatures was not always like the other boys. I launched my first "business" when I was about six years old. Vidabell laughed when she told Donna and Allie that I used to put these animals in boxes and then charge people a penny to look at them. According to my sister, it actually worked, and people (probably kids) paid the "viewing fee" regularly. The proceeds may have only paid for a three-cent can of soda here and there, but it was my own empire—my first "company." It became a partnership corporation shortly after that when a friend started helping me catch the displays as they scurried about the tumbleweeds, and we split the profits.

When my little museum wasn't in full operation, I tended to the creatures' needs the way you might expect a boy to, placing crickets in the box for a lizard's lunch and so on. But when one happened to die, I gave it a proper burial as well. I suppose even the lizards needed a good sermon once in a while. Vidabell remembers:

> When we lived in El Mirage, it was all desert. Our house was on the last road going out of town.... [Joe] would collect lizards and tadpoles and all kinds of stuff. Eventually they're gonna die, you know.
>
> Every time—and it happened a lot—every time he had a little lizard or something die, we had match boxes and he would put his little animal in there. He had an entire cemetery out in the backyard. We had a huge backyard and there was this little place everyone knew was Joe's little cemetery.
>
> He would put them in the matchbox, dig a little hole, and then he would take popsicle sticks, weave 'em together—or sometimes he would use a rubber band—like a cross, and he would put them in the ground and say a little prayer over 'em.... He was about...six or seven [years old].
>
> I wish I could remember what he said. Because I listened to

him a couple times. I didn't want him to know I was there. My window faced the backyard and I'd see him go out there, and once in a while I'd stand there secretly and listen to his sermons. It would just be a little thing. I'd go in and tell Mom, "Joe is gonna be a preacher."

Vidabell's prophecy would eventually come true.

And why not? Mom had been a preacher for about five years, and then had stopped about the time she had children. Grandma Horn, my dad's mother, had also been a preacher in the '30s during a time when women weren't kindly regarded as leaders in the church—but she was always well accepted everywhere she went. Grandpa Ardis McLaughlin was never a "pastor" in the professional sense, but he was often called in to preach at church (much like an associate pastor) when needed. Grandma Vida McLaughlin had been raised to rely on the Word as well, and though I don't remember any story of her taking the pulpit in a brick-and-mortar church setting, I have no doubt that her Methodist background prompted an on-the-spot sermon or ten when needy and weary pickers came through the campsite. I came from God-fearing roots, and even the lizards would be churched if I had anything to say about it at six years old. (My older brother Amil also grew up to be a preacher and has now been in full-time ministry as a church pastor for decades.)

Although this "business/preaching" of mine was a harbinger of ministerial days to come, before we get too busy painting me as a sweet, gentle, meek fellow who preached boyish sermons and ran barefoot around the cacti, it begs to be admitted that I had a mean streak also. Boy, did I sure put my sister through the wringer…

We didn't have money for much of anything in those days. In fact, in her letters during the 1950s, Mom talked about her concerns about obtaining groceries on a shoestring budget. Anything above and beyond a hot meal was a luxury—like the time Mom set aside money for weeks to get the ingredients to make us kids a chocolate pie. When she did, I started a pie fight. Vidabell shared this memory:

When we were really poor…Mom made a chocolate pie. She had talked about it for days, saying "I'm saving up enough money to make you guys a chocolate pie."

So she made this pie and gave us each a pretty good piece, and Amil was off one place and me and Joe were sitting across from each other…. Joe and I started throwing pieces at each other. Pie was goin' all over the place—the walls and table and everywhere—and about the time we were done having a pie fight, Mom came walking in.

We had never thought about that. And boy did we get in trouble!

It was a mess 'cause she gave us a pretty good-sized piece. Pie was just everywhere. Boy we got in trouble. Mom made us clean the whole thing up and then said we weren't getting any more chocolate pie.

"That's it. I don't got the money to be doin' this." And you know, we both got a spanking.…

We didn't get any chocolate pie for a long time. [Mom] would remind me of that all the time.… I never lived it down. "I saved this money forever to make you a chocolate pie, and you guys just ruined it, sittin' over there throwin' it at each other! Amil's over there savoring his. Boy…"

Somehow, despite our tight budget, Mom and Dad saved up enough money to buy Vidabell an official "Chatty Cathy" doll by Mattel, Inc. one birthday. It was an extraordinary expense for my parents. Vidabell waited and waited to open her presents, I'm sure thinking all the while that there was no way our family would ever have that kind of money.

To a little girl in the 1960s, Chatty Cathy wasn't just a doll, it was a companion. The world recalls the little television jingle: "Oh Chatty Cathy, oh Chatty Cathy, oh Mattel's famous talking doll! We'll pull the ring, and you say eleven different things!" Cathy would *actually speak to you* if you pulled the ring on her back, saying such things as, "I love you," "Please tell me a story," "Let's play house," and "Please change my dress."

What technology! Right? It was *such* a big deal!

Vidabell's dream became a reality when she opened that doll. Her begging and pleading with Mom and Dad for it had paid off. The doll was hers to own, to dress, to "raise," to mother, to share secrets with, to tuck into bed at night, and to show all the other girls that *Vidabell* of Mac's Trading Post was cutting edge enough to have a modern toy.

I don't know what possessed me, but I had it in my head that if I dipped that doll in tar, it would magically transform into a dark-skinned Cathy. (Perhaps I thought it would be like the characters people referred back then to as "tar babies," the African-American children in '60s cartoons? I realize that today that "tar baby" can be an offensive term, but in my childhood, it was a commonplace term, and my understanding of the term at around eight years old was innocent.) After I did in fact dip that doll in tar, I discovered that all I had "created" with my artistic endeavor was the irreversible destruction of my sister's favorite possession. A giant glob of goop with legs was all that materialized from my attempt to gift my sister with a unique African-American companion.

Recognizing that I had just ruined Vidabell's doll and that I wasn't the hero of the day, I ran straight to our outhouse, a small hole in the ground with a seat over it and four privacy walls around it, and threw Cathy in to meet a ghastly fate. I don't recall how long she stayed out there before my transgression was discovered, but once it was, *everyone* was mad. Grandpa McLaughlin made me fish her out to clean her off with some gasoline. I tried to, of course, but there was no fixing what I had done. Cathy was absolutely trashed.

As expected, I never lived that one down.

About ten years ago, I set out to right my wrongs and found several eBay auction listings for brand-new, first-edition Chatty Cathy dolls. Finding one in the box proved futile, as Mattel's "famous talking doll" is a collector's item and anything still in the box is long gone by now. Nonetheless, I continued to surf the listings until I found a doll in perfect condition. She still talked when the ring on her back was pulled. In a follow-up auction shortly afterward, I was able to win the box, separate from Cathy. Placing the two together, I sent them to my sister as an apology for my grand exploit so long ago. The gift was well received, and we haven't stopped laughing since.

I never allowed Vidabell to peacefully visit with her boyfriends while I was around. Mom had started letting my sister date at a young age, which wasn't uncommon in those days (Grandma Horn had married at the age of twelve), though usually the outings were chaperoned. I was about eight or nine when I started my shenanigans. Vidabell loathed my actions at the time, but they have become a string of endearing memories for her since. She always enjoys getting to tell on me now, as she did with Allie and Donna in front of their recorder:

I had a boyfriend named Danny...and I was just crazy about him. And your dad! Oh my gosh! He would terrorize me!

Anyway, me and my boyfriend was sitting in the car. He drove and had a really nice car and was super good-lookin'. We were going to leave and go to the café where I was working at the time. We got into kissing and hugging, you know how that is. He was telling me he loved me, I was telling him that too, and "You're so pretty," and, "You're so handsome." You know.

All of a sudden, I hear this voice from somewhere, you know, this [Vidabell speaks in a sing-song, mocking tone], "Oooo, I love you. Oooo, you are so pretty." And I said [she gasps], "That's my brother!" But I couldn't figure out where he was, because I couldn't see him. It continued again. "Oooo, I love you, oooo, muah muah muah [mock kissing sounds]." I opened up the door…and Joe came out from underneath the car. We coulda killed him! I had no idea he [was under the car]!

Like I said, we had decided to go down to the café where I worked and as things went on we decided not to. I think it was a "God thing," you know, [since Joe wasn't run over for a second time when we decided to leave for the café].…

Joe came running in the house saying, "I didn't do it!" He was yelling that before I even had a chance to tell Mom anything.… Mom knew when he did that that he was guilty, you know. She said, "Don't lie to me young man! I stood there and seen the whole thing!" [Vidabell explains that Mom had been standing at the kitchen window during the whole incident.] I said, "Mom, keep him in the house!"

No, dear readers, it doesn't stop there. Don't ask me why I tormented her like this, but I did so many times. Vidabell shares another occasion involving a boy named David:

My mom let me have a party at the house. She would let me do that occasionally with all my friends. And we had put down in these balloons these things you had to do. Either my boyfriend, or it was me, popped this balloon, and it said, "If you have a boyfriend or girlfriend, go around the house one time, and when you meet at the cooler, kiss." That was the deal you had to do.

So we're reading it, and I don't know where Joe was at. I had my teenage friends there, so I wasn't sure about Joe, but he heard it. This was back when we had coolers. There was no "air conditioning."

So [David] goes off in the same direction as me and we meet at the cooler. And this was back in the "old fashioned" days when people would close their eyes and then they'd kiss, so we got pretty close, and kinda put our arms around each other [her voice drops here, sounding odd and suspicious] and we kissed.

I looked at [David] and he looked at me at the same time, and Joe's hand went down like this. [She imitates a hand dropping quickly from the scene in a chopping motion.]

Your dad had put his hand up there, and we had actually kissed his hands from opposite sides! He was laughing and took off running. I was always shouting, "I'm tellin mom!" You know, because I was always just so aggravated with him....

It was just many incidents where he would absolutely terrorize me and my boyfriends.

Speaking of the cooler, here's a fun little doozy to remember me by, once again compliments of Vidabell's incredible memory:

Your dad was always doing something to scare me. He was always just thinking of ornery things to do. Like, one time, I came in and we had a cooler. He gets up on this chair and puts his hand down where the cooler was, and he just starts screaming bloody murder. I thought the cooler had got his hand, and I'm like, "Oh God! What am I gonna do! What am I gonna do!"

I was gonna turn the cooler off, but I thought, If his hand's in there—I don't know what to do! you know. He's like screaming bloody murder, like it's for real, and I…went to pick up the phone, and he went, "Nanny, nanny, nah nah." [Everyone in the background of the recording laughs.] He just took his hand out and went, "Nanny, nanny, nah nah." Yeah. He was a "nanny-na-na kid." Every time he was doing something ornery, he would say that to me, you know.

And then there was this time, the "hatchet story."… Mom would walk down that back alley to Grandma's house. Me and Joe was the only ones home. Dad was at work and I don't know where Amil was. He was older, and me and Joe would buddy around. Your dad got mad at me about something and went and got the hatchet. He said he was gonna "get me" and he was doing like this [Vidabell mimics a chopping motion with her hand clamped around an invisible hatchet].

He was like ten or so. Old enough to know better.

He started chasing me around with it. He almost got me a couple times, and I don't know if he realized how bad he coulda hurt me! And I was runnin' and runnin' and he was chasin' me with a stinkin' hatchet!

He denied that story for years! For years and years and years, and then finally when he was in Crescent City, he told the story.

I don't remember [what the original argument was that day]. He just got mad at me about something I did, or I wouldn't play with him, or something. Scared me half to death! I just knew I was gonna die or get my back cut open. I was screaming and yelling. I thought I heard mom coming and Joe runs and hides the hatchet. Mom comes through the back door and I said, "Mom! Joe chased me with a hatchet!"

And he says, "I did not! I. Did. Not. I did not do it."

He always denied everything.... He didn't get in trouble because she hadn't seen it, but she gave him a little lecture about how if he did do something like that, "You could really hurt your sister," and that kinda thing. "I better never catch you doin' something like that," you know.

Some of the things I got away with were inherent in being the youngest one in the family. That is likely true of many children, but I milked it. I know I did. I may not have the most reliable memory when it comes to what I did or didn't do, but I know what I was like, and I was certainly capable of that. Vidabell remembers the specifics:

Your dad was the baby of the family, and he may not admit this, but he was the spoiled one, because Mom and Dad said, "You kids are gonna learn how to work. You're gonna go to the fields every summer when you're outta school and chop cotton. You can have some of the money you made but not all of it. You can have a little bit."

So we go out to chop cotton, and me and Amil have to go and [work hard] but Joe is sharing a row with Mom, so she's really doing all the work and Joe's just kinda piddling around, and then when they go into Johnson grass—which is really hard to get out of the ground, because the ground was hard—then me and Amil would have to go and help them, and Joe was just piddling around! [Everyone in the background of the recording laughs.]

I promise. It was so unfair. [At this, the background laughter becomes hysterical for a moment and eventually tapers off.]

Another thing [he] used to do that isn't written down—and this is famous! Amil knows it's true. I know it's true. Mom knew it was true. Your dad would fake being sick because he hated school… [Vidabell imitates:] "Oh, I'm sick! I'm sick! My stomach hurts! I got a fever! I gotta go lay down! I'm sick!" I mean, he was really quite an actor, your dad.

Then Mom would go in and say, "Oh, you really are sick, you better stay home from school today." And then he'd always tell her, "I need a hamburger and a chocolate shake and a wind-up toy." [Again, everyone in the background laughs.]

So, Mom would go get him a hamburger, a chocolate shake, and a wind-up toy at TGMY, which was just up the road in Young Town. But if me and Amil got sick? No can do. We didn't get stuff. We didn't get special treatment. But Joe was the baby and he always got a wind-up toy.

He had so many wind-up toys! He had this little monkey that banged cymbals together and he…would always get [another] one when he was "sick."

And then, Mom caught onto it, that he was faking it. "He's playing sick an awful lot." So she went to send him to school one day, and he told her he was sick, and she said, "Naw, I'm getting tired of this You're always 'sick,' and you're going to school."

Then [later that day] the nurse calls and says, "Your son's runnin' a temperature." He really was sick and Mom didn't believe him. So…she had to go to school and get him.

And of course he got— Guess what he got! Hamburger, chocolate shake, and a wind-up toy. [Laughter.]

When I got older, I worked at Effie's Café, and Effie was really strict to work for. Everything [you ate] went on a tab and then they take it out of your check. Well Joe didn't realize that; he was just a kid. I wanna say he was like twelve or something. He would come down there with his friends, Ronnie…and sometimes he would have two friends… He thought because I worked there I got [food] for free. So he'd say, "Two steak sandwiches, two chocolate shakes, and two large fries." I'd say, "Okay." And I'd always do it for him.

I never said anything to him. Never in my life did I ever say anything to him. One time, after having his businesses started… he came in here and he said, "Hey, I've been meaning to ask you, when you used to work for Effie's Café and I would come in with my friends and get all that stuff, did that go on your tab?"

I said, "Absolutely, it went on my tab. Effie would have killed anyone giving anything away for free. Yeah, it came out of my paycheck. But, you know, I didn't care, you were my little brother."

Even though we would fight we loved each other. I loved him. I always loved him.

Like with the Chatty Cathy incident, years passed, but eventually, I paid Vidabell back for those steak sandwiches, chocolate shakes, and large fries. She was always so kind to forgive me for all the foolishness

I pulled on her. What a gracious person, Vidabell. I don't deserve this feedback, but she gave it nonetheless:

> I always loved my little brother, Joe…. Joe and I always had a special bond, even though he would pull off a lotta things when he was younger. But now they're memories I really like to think about. Joe's been a great brother to me. A great brother. I've talked to him so many times and he's helped me through a great deal. A great deal. Yeah.
>
> I always could tell Joe anything, and no matter how crazy it sounds, he would believe me, and believe in me. He's very understanding and sympathetic. He encourages me and always has. He's always been there for me. I'm glad to have a brother that believes in me.

I guess at some point I made up for the things that money couldn't replace. I didn't, however, ever learn to like school.

When I was in either the end of the sixth grade or the beginning of the seventh, I dropped out of school. Mom and Dad had gotten a divorce, and it was up to Amil and myself to support Mom. We were lucky to have the campsite, or else we may have been in bigger trouble. My very first job, not counting the lizard museum, was shining shoes outside "Cozy Corners," a hamburger joint everybody in El Mirage knew about in those days. I never wasted time pursuing any work I could get my hands on, and we made a living somehow. Nothing was ever easy, but on the other hand, nothing was ever too hard for us to handle as a family.

At the beginning of this chapter, I mentioned that my mother had been pregnant *six* times in a short period of years. After I was born, she became pregnant one last time. The pregnancy included many difficulties, and my baby sister was born at just six months. Her name was Rose, and Vidabell remembers that those in the family who had a chance to see the preemie referred to her as the most beautiful baby they had ever seen. Rose lived for only a few hours, and her death broke Mom's heart. She started having terrible, haunting dreams, so Dr. Shackleford performed an autopsy in order to figure out why Rose hadn't survived. He learned that she had been born with a large section of her brain missing. Had she lived, she would have been a vegetable, brought into the very life that the doctors had warned my mother that could have happened with *me*. Mom had taken the risk again, choosing not to abort, and in the end, when Rose did not make it, it was God—not an operation to terminate—that took her home. Between that fact and the knowledge that Rose would never have been able to lead a normal life, my mother was able to accept her death. However, Mom never got over the pain of that loss. The truth is, that baby very well could have been me. I lived in spite of medical and scientific opinion when I shouldn't have—*twice*. (And again I say: The hand of God, perhaps? Credit where credit is due.)

I never had a little sister, and there are times I would have loved to. But I *did* have the best family anyone could have asked for.

I remained close to all of them, including my Dad, who even after the divorce was *always* there for me. In the 1990s, Dad and his brother, Billy, had gone deer hunting. Midway through their trip, Dad spotted a deer at the bottom of a steep hill and told Billy he was going in after it. Billy was disabled, and therefore could not accompany Dad further. According to Billy's memory of the incident, Dad wandered for a bit in an attempt to close in on his prize, and then, abruptly, he lifted his hand to the sky as if reaching for something that wasn't there, then fell to the ground. Billy called 911, but by the time anyone was able to descend into the canyon and reach Dad, he had already passed on.

The news devastated me, but I recall that there were some lead-up circumstances that point to the idea that Dad had sensed it might be about his time to go. He had been speaking of God and Scripture increasingly, and said a few other things that suggested he was getting his earthly affairs in order. This didn't alleviate the pain of his sudden disappearance from my life, but it did lessen the blow because I knew that, in the end, he was serious about Christ. He had always been a believer, but his increased devotion was a comfort. I have no doubt that he's with the Lord now, and even though I miss him greatly and his death was terribly sad to go through, I know my separation from him is temporary.

My mother was a constant in my life, and despite the miles between us when I left home later on, I always kept in close touch. Our phone calls were frequent, and I took advantage of any chance I got to drive out and visit with her for several days.

When I bought the tickets for Allie and Donna to take their recorder to Arizona and speak with my relatives, my mother was still alive. In the days just prior to their flight out, after having fallen and broken her hip, Mom's health began to decline rapidly. Needless to say, their trip suddenly became less about interviews and more about being there for their grandmother. While Allie and Donna were packing and heading to the airport, my son and I were a day ahead of them, driving as quickly as we could to be there with her in what the doctors were referring to as her final hours. By the time I got there, she had already passed on, but I got to see her, hold her hand, thank her for everything she meant to me, and tell her goodbye. Allie and Donna did not arrive in time to see her, but they had already been scheduled to be in Arizona for a week, and their assistance to their Aunt Vidabell (who had been living with Mom) was important in the days following Mom's passing. (What had started out as a fun visit to get "the dirt" on me as a boy took a tragic turn.) My brother Amil came out as well, and we all spent time together reflecting upon Mom's memory. Vidabell welcomed the recorder and the list of questions, as they provided her with a healthy and meaningful distraction. (Amil was not available for interview because, in addition to dealing with the sadness of Mom's death, he has been tending to a very sick grandson, whose side he rarely leaves.)

I owe my life to my father because of the day he took me from that hospital and brought me to Dr. Shackleford's. I owe my life to my mother because of the day she decided that, in order to save me, she had to risk letting me—or herself—die. My parents' footprints have changed too many lives to count. I owe the value of my life to all of them: Grandma, Grandpa, Mom, Dad, Amil, Vidabell, and so many others in my extended family whose roles in my life have shaped me and the footprint I will leave behind in this world.

Throughout my children's lives, as they will personally attest, I have countless times uttered the words: "All that matters is God and family." God gave me my family, and my family gave me joy and shape. When I grew into a young man, God added to my family through my current wife, Nita.

And it is to those details we will now turn. But before we do, I want to leave a last thought here for the reader.

There were those in my childhood who didn't believe in me. Some thought I was "as good as gone" before I ever reached birth or the age of five. To others, I appeared as a scrawny little desert urchin catching lizards and tormenting my sister. My *family*, however, never stopped believing in me, even when I didn't deserve it.

You have likely heard it said, "Keep your friends close, and your enemies closer."

Nah. That's secular thinking.

Keep your family close, and God closer. Remember to always give thanks to the One who provides. Be thankful for the time you have with those who love you. Relish the happy thoughts, and grow beyond the ripples. Don't spend precious time in this life holding grudges or harboring anger against a loved one when you can repair and restore instead. Think twice before you write off the value of another human life, whether that be an unborn baby, a severely wounded boy in the hospital, an annoying neighborhood kid who builds ridiculous "speed ramps," or a little brother who continuously terrorizes you.

And for heaven's sake, don't dip your sister's brand-new doll in tar.

It won't work out.

Three

The Boy in the Ridiculous Hat

ollowing my parents' divorce, I spent most of my waking hours tending to the needs of the family. By the time I was thirteen, I had landed a management position at the Circle One Feedlot. I ran heavy equipment, drove big trucks, controlled the mill (as well as countless other duties), and had twenty dump truck drivers who worked under me as I operated the largest payloader made at the time. In those days, Arizona law allowed one to obtain a provisional driver's license at the age of thirteen and drive on country roads (or on main roads if an adult was present), so I was able to get around. I usually just went wherever I wanted, regardless of whether an adult was with me, and as a result, I traveled wherever the job required.

During the few recreational hours I had, I was usually up to no good.

I didn't understand or respect the treasure trove I had been born with. The desert was simply packed with historical significance at every turn. Dad used to get paid to ride a horse along the fence lines of Bard Ranch, where he gained an upright reputation with the Native Americans in the area. Having been invited to the reservations, I scouted the outskirts and found all kinds of relics from the past. These precious items are all buried under modern construction now, but when I was a kid, they were everywhere: arrowheads, clay pots, and precious heirlooms of a lost era. One of these heirlooms was, for a short time, in my possession. It was made of fired clay and was shaped like the head of an Indian chief. I was far too curious for my own good when I discovered that the head rattled when shaken.

Here's how dumb I was, right?

Before using any investigative strategy to determine whether the head might have held any value (monetarily or culturally), I busted it open to see what was inside. A perfectly round, beautiful, blue rock fell into my hand. To the Indians, this was a rare gem. To me?

A marble.

It made a good shooter, too, because of its shape.

Years later, an antiquarian and I were talking about this find, and he told me the Indians may have created a clay head for a beloved chief when he passed on and filled the hollow sculpture with a precious gemstone before burying it with the departed. Whether the stone itself would have been appraised at great value is beside the fact that the antique head— which was probably modeled after a famous Indian leader—had been, as the antiquarian put it, "enormously valuable."

Marble!

What silly thing to do. Sadly, it would not be the last priceless and historical artifact that would be lost in the folds of time while I was hunting for "toys" in the sand.

When my sister married and moved out, Mom and I lived quietly for a time on Grandpa's camp. Mom got a job working as a cook at a quaint burger place called Sir George's. I was constantly running around the area barefoot, and one day, I saw smoke rising from the distance. The dry, hot Arizona flora was, and still is, a breeding ground for spreading flame, and certainly a fire close to my home while Mom was at work was something that I had to investigate. Upon closer inspection, I saw that a house had caught fire. I walked around the house and glanced in all the windows to be sure no one was still inside before I left to call the fire department.

Sure enough, I heard a noise scuffling about inside.

I couldn't tell if the noise-maker was animal or human, and the smoke on the other side of the glass was so black and so thick that I was sure whoever or whatever it was on the inside was likely gasping for air and couldn't shout for help. Thinking fast, I considered my next move. Breaking a window would be a last resort, since exiting through the window from inside would require agility and height that a trapped individual may not be able to manage. Breaking through the sliding glass door made far more sense.

Running to the door, I lifted my leg and struck it with the force of a black belt and the urgency of a fireman. There was an immediate backdraft effect, and the glass exploded like a bomb, lacerating my lower leg. (I don't remember any person or animal coming out of that house, but my sister seems to remember a small, white dog.) The smoke poured from the door, creating a bubble of visibility, and I was able to see to the back of the house to make sure nobody else was trapped inside. Stunned by the blow, I picked the largest pieces of glass from my foot and made my way to get help to fight the flames.

Vidabell was living with her husband in Phoenix when she heard about the incident. By this time, she had a little girl named Lavida (yes, another generation of "Vida" names), and she brought her over to visit me a few days after the fire. Mom was at Sir George's when Vidabell took one look at my foot and grimaced.

"Joe, your foot is *really* infected!" she said.

I didn't listen.

She continued to go on and on about the marvel that was festering from the wound. "Joe!" she said, pointing to these bizarre lines on my leg. "That's blood poisoning! I'm taking you to the doctor!"

"Nah, it's just swollen. It's fine. It's just hurtin' a little bit, but it'll be okay."

No warning from her changed my mind. I was set in my belief that it would heal on its own.

Turns out, I could have been an amputee.

Vidabell, who had given up on trying to convince me, ran to a phone and called Mom, interrupting her at work. This wasn't something we would have normally done if it hadn't been an emergency, so Mom stopped cooking and took the call.

"Mom, Joe's foot is really, *really* bad. It's *super* infected, and he will NOT let me take him to the doctor. He *will not* do it. The only person he's gonna listen to is you!"

Mom dropped everything and came home at once. Between the time Vidabell had called her and the time Mom arrived to take me to a medical center, Vidabell got up close and personal with my leg. She remembers:

I don't think he realized how severe it was. When I really got to lookin' at it after I called [Mom] there was several places that were— Well, one of the [blood poisoning lines] was tracing up to his knee, and several other places were starting up. [If he hadn't gone with Mom to the doctor,] he would have easily lost his foot, and possibly his leg up to the knee.

I was placed on antibiotics in the nick of time, and eventually, I retained full use of that leg. I have Mom and Vidabell to thank for that. Not all of the trouble I got into in the desert was as heroic, however.

I had a friend named Ronnie. We were inseparable. Our friendship had been immediate and strong from the moment we had met; our interests and fascinations were complementary, and the desert was our oyster.

Allie and Donna were able to make a daytime road trip to Arkansas to meet with Ronnie and get his memories of those days on record. He, too, remembers our unique adolescent alliance:

Me and your dad always connected. You didn't feel a pull, you didn't feel a push. We just connected. We influenced each other, obviously, but we were kids. We both experienced difficulties in our lives [around that time]. My father had left, we moved three or four times, and then we moved to a rental place—a project type setting—just me, my mother, and my brother. That's how I met your father....

This was probably in 1966 or '67. I was about twelve or thirteen years old, and we lived at the foothills of White Tank Mountains. At any rate, I ran around barefooted and hopping from shadow to shadow because it was so hot in Arizona, in El Mirage.... In my trips back and forth to the store, I ran into your dad....

At that time when you went to get a Coke, I remember the small bottles were a nickel. They were in that process where they went from a nickel to a dime and included the deposits. And Joe would go buy these little Cokes and he would fill them with peanuts, and then he'd walk around and bob his head around like [Ronnie mimics a young hipster "cool cat" routine and everyone in the background of the recording laughs]. But he was at the store and we talked and it was a casual thing. Joe said, "Yeah, you know, come on over to my place bla bla bla."...

I went to visiting him a lot in the very beginning and met his mother and father, Clarence. At this time, Sally was [still living] at home. I said, "Ya got any games?"

He said, "Nope, no games. I got chess, though. Do you know how to play?"

"Nope."

"I'll teach you."

From that moment, as Ronnie remembers, we were the best of buddies our side of the Mississippi. I taught him how every piece on that board played, and he was at my house constantly for another match. From my place to his and back, he was hopping sandy hot spots and dodging tumbleweeds, all the while practicing the fine arts of greenhorn-Joe chess, not even home yet before he was planning his next visit: "So I would get home [from school] and tell my mom, 'I'm gonna go see Joe!' It got so bad that my mom thought I was obsessed with the chess guy. But we were just kids and it was fun."

When our chess kick had run its course, we started spending more time outdoors hammering away on random piles of wood in an attempt to make "go-carts," crudely attaching little wheels and rigging up rookie steering, which we would then drive over ramps and run down into the gulleys and streams. When we weren't begging for a nail in the knee-cap via our sketchy-at-best, wild-West wagon-trail adventures, we were hunting lizards or poking cacti. Our escapades stretched into the late hours on many occasions. Ronnie relates:

I remember there was a curfew. I think nine o'clock or so, and everybody had to be in. This was the time the mosquito truck still ran around. It was this big ol' fog machine that would drive around and fog the streets to kill mosquitos in the evening hours. It didn't bother us at all, but they did this at a certain hour and there was a curfew.

Well anyway, when we ran wild, when it got dark, we didn't really have supper, we just skipped it or whatever. Kids, you know. We ran around in this town in El Mirage—and it was safer then than it is now, but it was dangerous then, too—but we would carry sticks because of dogs… Wherever we were going we would carry sticks because we were tough guys. We were ready for the [other kids or teens in the area] to jump on us! We were ready to stick up for each other. We were just tight at that time, you know. But when that happened, Joe was always the first to run! [Everyone laughs.] I mean, he was just GONE! [Ronnie makes a sound like a cartoonish retreat-whistle.]

However, he would surprise me constantly and take the lead on some adventure and I would go along with him on a whim, but we found ourselves sometimes out late at night. We weren't really destructive. I don't think so, anyway. I mean, one time, we were in somebody's backyard—I don't remember why—and I remember this porch light coming on and us lying down in the shadows. We were in the dark spots. Joe did not move; I did not move. How that guy did not see us is a miracle, but were just there till he shut the light off and went back in....

Joe's dad, Amil, Amil's friends, my brother Charles, and all my distant relatives and family in and around California scattered around that area—they all had things they were doing, so it was always just me, my mother, and Joe. Sally had went to stay at, I'm thinking it was her mother's, Sally's mom's, and they [Sally and Clarence] were kinda separating. I thought, Oh no. They're separating. They're having problems, you know. I had lost my father as well, so we always had kind of a connection there in my mind...and at nighttime we would still be out and we were ducked down around buildings. There was a curfew where his mother was, too. I recall one time—and I think it was Amil's car, I'm not sure—but I remember us taking his hubcap because we were mad at him or something. Joe was just, "Yeah! We got his hupcap!" That kinda stuff.

I thought I was on the top of the world when I got my hands on a minibike, but as Ronnie remembers, after I had to replace the clutch on that dumb thing for the fourth time, I returned to travel by foot.

It was the late '60s and there was a lot of hardcore hippies in the parks, you know. We would be in and out of the park but they would just scare me to death because I have pictures in my mind, still, of what I saw going on and it just scared me to death because of the openness, guys screamin' about acid, you know. But we weren't into that. We knew it was there, but we weren't involved in that crowd.

Once in a while we would sneak behind a building and smoke a cigarette, but Joe was really into Ray Stevens' music— you know, that "squirrel got loose in the church" guy—and he was always playing records and laughing. We had a lot of fun.

Another year or so passed and I was trading in my Ray Steven's "Squirrel Went Berserk" album for Iron Butterfly's "In-A-Gadda-Da-Vida" and Fleetwood Mac's "Black Magic Woman," but at my worst in the late 1960s I was still relatively harmless, despite the fact that the chip on my shoulder was developing right on schedule. Ronnie and I were still close, but with what my family was going through, I found more and more of my time was spent tending to things at home, so we weren't together as often as before. When we did bump into each other, we picked things up right where we had left off. To me, it's actually quite sad to think that today, "devious" behavior is what it is. For Ronnie and me, "devious" was comparatively innocent:

I met Joe going or coming somewhere and found out he quit school. His hair was all long, you know. We went from chewing gum and baseball posters to black lights and fluorescent posters, but it's not a dark scene. He quit school and then a few times we went there just when school was out. We met some girls and one was in my class and she had gone to an Oasis Drive-In for like a dollar a car-load. In those days people were crammed in the trunk for places like that.

Anyway this girl's brother wouldn't take us along and my brother couldn't take us, so we climbed over the fence, over the gate, and we're out watching the movie with these girls. As devious as this was, it progressed to the point that we ended up getting our hands on a car or something somehow and going out to their house and meeting them there in person—we were around fifteen at this time or so—and come to find out, it was a girl's home where they had foster kids. And oh were they strict! Those foster parents were all over us! [Laughter in background.]

We went to Phoenix one time, down Grand Avenue, and we went on a trampoline where you pay a dollar an hour to jump or something. Then we went to Mr. Lucky's. I don't know what was motivating Joe for this adventure, but I was just along for the ride. It was a lounge setting, and I remember peeking in the door. Joe was a little taller, so he could move a little farther in before they escorted him out, but I was shorter. Joe was obsessed with going there....

Afterwards we found ourselves back out on the road, back out in town, crossing through neighborhoods, taking shortcuts, making our way back home, crossing through sun city, Young-town, and that night when it was late we went crossing the Agua Fria riverbed there.... And this is a big bridge. We actually walked along the ledge under the bridge sometimes as kids crossing the river there. So we're down at the riverbed and we crossed over one side where there was a housing development right at the top of this twenty-five- or thirty-foot bluff. I don't know how tall it was, it mighta been bigger. And right in a hole on the side of there was some ducks that were nesting. There mighta been two or three of them.

I had my old trusty shotgun with me. I still have it. I've had this shotgun since I was seven years old. Us kids grew up having shotguns and knives. I could go outta the house carrying this thing. My mother would just, you know, "Be careful! Have fun!" and there was no problem with it. No questions asked. Just outta sight, outta mind. My mother had to know that we were just up to anything and everything. However, we're in this riverbed and we see this big ol' white duck. Right there. Me and Joe and whoever else was with us, we were kinda scattered a little bit, but we're in close proximity, and I [Ronnie mimics aiming] POW! I shoot this duck and feathers are flyin' everywhere. This big ol' guy comes walkin' up to the edge of the hill.

He goes, "Are you shootin' my ducks!?"

Well, I laid the gun down real quick and shouted, "No! It was a guy in a truck! Some guy in a jeep!" you know, and he's lookin' around. [Laughter in background.] So we got past that episode, but it was that close. Everything was always "that close." We were always getting away with everything.

Of course, the Ronnie days wouldn't be complete without telling one really bird-brained stunt I pulled. Of all things we did together, of all the things I ever did in my childhood, this was the worst…and, as usual, *I* had started it.

There was a church property around the block from Cozy Corner Café, and on its lot was a little bungalow building located a distance from the main church building. The bungalow had been abandoned for a *long* time, and, by the looks of it, its only remaining purpose was as a crash pad for vandals and what Ronnie called the "hardcore hippies." Ronnie described the place as being in a "total trashed state; there was cusswords written all over the wall, there was naked pictures…it was just filthy stuff! The room must have been abandoned for some time and it was just a filthy place. There may have been defecation in there, who knows, it was just a nasty, nasty place." Ronnie recalls the details better than I do about how I saw fit to rectify the eyesore:

Okay, here's the episode. Joe was a very good pool player, by the way. He could bank shots! I could too, but he was a really good pool player. There were some times I beat him, and oooh, that would make him furious! [Laughter in background.] It cost a quarter to play a game of pool and we would get a pocket full of quarters at the Cozy Corner. It was like a little café on one end but they had a pool table and pinball machines.

However this one time, we were either on our way to his house, or—well, we didn't really have no place in mind. But we're goin' up the alley off of the beaten path, off the highway, and Joe wanders into this building [the bungalow on the church property]. I had never been in here, but we just go on into this open door…

We're exploring.… Joe is standing over here, the door is over here—and I remember this all so clearly—there was a window here with a raggedy curtain and Joe's got a lighter. And he goes [Ronnie mimics me as a kid starting the lighter and holding it to the curtain; he makes a "fshh" sound]. He does this towards it, and I'm over on the far end…and when I turn away, I lit the curtain on my end. I remember lighting that curtain, right? But I know that Joe started this, okay? However [Ronnie makes a "run-for-it" clap motion with his hand and another cartoon retreat-whistle sound]—and Joe's gone! Joe is gone! And I'm the last one out, but when I left, the curtain is just "fssshhhh," right?

Out the door! Down the alley! And we got to Cozy Corner where we're now playin' pool.

Now, for a few seconds here, bein' kids, I had completely forgotten about what we had just done. Until we hear the sirens. [Ronnie mimics a siren outside.] So here's the sirens, and Joe's... lookin' over at me like, "We know what's goin' on, we know what's goin' on." So I'm kinda hangin' out, Joe makes this move for the door, I follow him out, and Joe just disappears! So help me—Joe disappears!

I'm standing there with all these people around with a fire goin' on, and I'm just lookin' at this humongous fire. I mean it was big!... And these people are saying, "Yeah, we saw kids running!" and they're lookin' at me. I just played it off real good 'cuz I was never suspected since we were never into that kinda stuff....

We really were above all of this usually, okay, but the thing that stays true to me was what was on our mind at the time.... What's important to realize is that, in our minds, we were doing a justice! Because this just was not right for a church property to be like that. In our minds it just shouldn't be tolerated.

Yes, that was definitely the worst. Yes, I tucked my tail and ran once again. And yes, it was all my idea. According to Ronnie, *many* things were my idea: "Joe would say, 'Let's go!' and away we'd go, you know. I didn't even think about it. I didn't think about how we were gonna get there [or what we were getting into]."

Eventually—*sadly*—after my parents had officially split up and the obligations at home and work were mounting to the point that our little misadventures had to take a back seat to responsibility, I started seeing Ronnie less and less frequently. We would see each other rarely, and when we did it was a brief exchange as I was headed off to work or home to check on Mom. I didn't realize then how much I would miss hanging around with my buddy—or that I would retain the memories of those days in the desert for the rest of my life to the point that Ronnie would nearly become a celebrity to my kids. When he left one day, he was just gone. He relates:

> I never did say goodbye to Joe. I was traveling around a lot with my brothers and we eventually lost touch. I remember when I moved away from there that was in my mind, though. I remember just thinking about how Joe was involved with his new family now, and he had a lot going on.

But as tragic as all this sounds, it wasn't *quite* over, as I would discover forty-plus years later... How fun it was for me when Donna was compiling the notes for this book and suddenly sent me an email with a link to Ronnie's Facebook account! It blew my mind! I recognized him instantly. He had a few years behind him, but it was definitely the same Ronnie.

Right away I contacted him, got his phone number, and gave him a call. Within that first conversation we agreed that he would bring his motorcycle out to my place two days later...only this time it wasn't for chess, sketchy go-cart construction, catching lizards, or bringing vigilante justice to vandalized buildings.

No. No kid stuff. We're grown-ups now. The bar had to be raised. This time, we were going to blow up the world!

While I was working on this book, Ronnie came to visit me to watch fireworks. This was the first time we had seen each other in more than forty years. Here, we're pictured waiting for dark to "blow up the world"—as my family would say. We always do July 4 up big at my place.

What a cool time that was, "blowing up the world" together, catching up while we lit things on fire, and I saw what a neat guy he had turned out to be. People frequently think about that neighborhood kid they grew up next to, wondering what direction his or her life took, and hoping the report would be positive. Sometimes childhood friends *do* connect later, and the situation is less than ideal. I thank God that Ronnie turned out to be such a class act. He now lives with his wife in Arkansas and spends every minute of his free time ministering to and visiting with the retired elderly in his community.

I have to admit, I *was* aware that I had possessed a knack for starting shenanigans and then running away, but hearing about it from Ronnie and later learning what he said in his interview with Allie and Donna, I realized I was guilty far more often than I had remembered. I suppose, then, I deserved what I got when I was the one left holding the guilty bag...

At times I went looking for trouble, but on rare occasions, it found me. One acquaintance was especially wild (and for the sake of his privacy, we will call him Timmy). During one extravagant outing, this buddy Timmy had stolen a car and thought it would be a fun idea to drive like a madman all over the sandy desert with it. He came to pick me up so he wouldn't have to relish his joyride alone. He not only hit the cacti we approached at rampant speeds; he *aimed at* them. From one mound of tumbleweeds into the next cactus, into the next giant bush, and so on, he sped directly into obstacles for sport until the car had been beatten to a mangled scrap of steel. Before long, the front end of the stolen vehicle was smoking wildly, and we were spotted by law enforcement down the highway we were traveling back to El Mirage.

Immediately, the cop put on his lights, pulled us over, discovered that the car was stolen, and handcuffed us. We were both arrested and taken to the El Mirage jailhouse.

I remember sitting in a small front room of the police station while the policeman gathered information from me. He had removed both of our handcuffs, but he hadn't yet spoken to Timmy. I cooperated, telling him who I was and my connection to the joyride, despite the fact that I knew I was going to have a guilty spot on my record as a result. As we talked, the man interviewing us got up and went into the adjoining room to retrieve something. Timmy saw that as his opportunity to make a run for it. Without a word, he jumped up from his seat, bolted for the door, and fled from the building.

When the officer came back a moment later, he said, "Where's the other kid?"

"He ran out that door," I said matter-of-factly.

Timmy was never caught for his stunt, and I took the rap. I had a criminal record now. What a deal that was. (Note, however, that because I was a minor at the time, when I turned eighteen with no other legal marks against me, the crime was expunged from my record.)

As the years passed, I grew to be quite the ladies' man. And by that, I don't mean that I was getting anyone pregnant or ruthlessly breaking hearts, mind you, but I had a player's streak.

Picture this: I was a regular James Dean of the sands, clad in the most hip and mod sunglasses of the day, wooing ladies, and whipping my flowing mane in the face of danger. My jeans were torn at the knee and the sleeves of my shirt were shredded, revealing my tough, cutting-edge tattoos as well as my tan and muscular arms. Every time I appeared, the sounds of Steppenwolf's "Born to Be Wild" floated in from out of nowhere, heads turned, and the world's brakes were slammed like a slow-motion scene from a Hollywood film. My very presence caused some to faint. I was bad...*so* bad.

Wait...

No. That wasn't it. That's what *I* thought of myself.

Ahem. Let's start again...

Picture this: I was a regular, skinny, desert kid, clad in the most ridiculous limp-brimmed hat you've ever seen (seriously, that hat was stupid-looking), and I was always talking smack. With every smile, my crooked teeth were revealed—surrounded by a frame of sunburnt straw that I thought was hair. The "danger" I got into was typical, childish, show-off recitals, and my clothes were run-of-the-mill hand-me-downs, revealing my scraggly, lanky limbs. I had a fresh batch of "tattoos" that some friend of mine bestowed upon me, but neither he nor I had known what we were doing, so the tattoos ended up being the weird, nonsensical, green scratch marks that I now have to live with. (These "tattoos" are visible on my arms in the picture with Ronnie a few pages back.) I never had a theme song, I didn't turn heads, and the world never went slow-mo when I walked onto the scene. My very presence caused some to sigh in frustration. I was ignorant...*so* ignorant.

To be honest, I can't fathom why I was popular with girls, what they saw in me, or why in the world they ever gave me a second glance when there were so many other handsome and intelligent suitors in Arizona. I talked big, acted tough, and always wore that goofy-looking sunhat that swung around my head like a dead fish. It sheltered my scalp from the sun, but that's about all it was good for. Between my bare feet, frequently bare chest, and long "hippie" hair jutting out of that unreasonable hat, I was a match made in heaven for someone looking to date an oblivious dork.

Nonetheless, despite whatever argument might be launched regarding the sanity of the girls around me, I did somehow manage to get a lot of attention when it came to females.

I remember being quite the charmer in one setting, then finding myself in a completely different social group later the same afternoon, flirting my way into the hearts of the hopefuls so that by bedtime I had at least two or three girls convinced of my interest on any given day. My job, my Mom, and the rest of my family had my real attention. My hobnobbing was more for sport, but the young ladies were none the wiser.

As far as each was concerned, I only had eyes for them. Maybe they were willing to see beyond the foolish, adolescent exterior. Maybe they needed to be flattered and I was the one dropping lines. Maybe they were young and impressionable. Maybe they were just lonely. Maybe, no matter what generation, teenage girls can be swooned by that young guy who acts like the leader of the pack even when he's not. I'll never understand *why*, but I had no lack of girlfriends at any point in my teen years.

What a mystery this has always been to me.

I was oftentimes the gossip of "girl corners," and the giggling whenever I was around let me know I had the upper hand to smooth talk. And then—*Pow! Zing!*—I'd drop my juvenile one-liners and walk away with a wink-and-gun finishing touch that placed me right back where I thought I deserved to be: in the center of female attention.

Bam. Worked every time.

What a punk.

However, I *never* truly got anything out of all that. Not really. Not *deeply*. There was a lot of visiting, flirting, flattering, laughing, and "shootin' the breeze" going on, but at the core of my being, I wasn't fulfilled with anything hailing from my social groups. It was a daily façade. A role I was playing in this ongoing, menial drama called life. That much could be seen in how often I retreated from the crowds and just…thought about stuff.

About life, about purpose, about the meaning of existence, about whether or not there really was an all-powerful "Being" in the sky… I thought about everything. On the rare occasion I tried to bring the others in my teenage circle into a conversation about the mysteries of this planet or anything spiritual, I was either met with another fit of giggles from my silly entourage, or I got the faux-transcendence response that was trendy at the time, amounting to: "Yeah, groovy. I hear ya, Joe. I mean, what does it all *mean*? You know what I mean?" And then, there I was, straight back to the hip kid on the block.

My "go-to."

Pow. Zing. Bam.

Blah.

I don't intend to poke fun, because I *was* surrounded by many quality people, but I never once connected to anyone, especially any girls, on a profound level. I was the "cool cat" when I was around them also, which would not have inspired that side of them to come out around me even if it was there. I'm sure they were projecting themselves around me in the light I was demanding them to by my own behavior. They were going along with the game, though, and it was all so lonely.

So, when the seemingly ceaseless hours of banter ended, I would go off alone into some corner of the world and ponder.

The sky was an anomaly to me. That sun… It was just a giant ball of flaming gas so far away, yet burning so intensely that it could make the sand on the ground in Arizona hot enough to blister the skin. What was that all about? Who made it? Did it create itself from a rotating gas cloud, like scientists said? If so, that was amazing—almost too amazing to be feasible, actually. Much of science seemed that way, and the mathematic relationship between space, the universe, and all living beings on the planet—and how each worked together exactly how they needed to without a hitch in order to randomly and autonomously arrange itself *by chance*— was a hard "truth" to wrap my brain around. There just had to be more to the story of origin. And the sky at night! When the sun was no longer limiting my ability to fully cast my eyes on this vast, massive, cosmic reality, I could take in the stars like an enormous and sparkling blanket above the world and know that this thing was so big that every single person in the country could look up at that same instant and see the same stars. Had that happened by some nearly incomputable accident also?

Church people sometimes said "God" made it all. As unbelievable as that may be, an ultimate Power above who could snap His fingers and bring it all together had some merit, as it canceled out unfathomably lucky mathematics and random chance entirely, replacing them with *purpose*.

I liked to think my life had a purpose. I liked to think that when I left this world someday, I would leave a footprint behind that would amount to more than just a few laughs to people who would eventually cease to exist when their temporal lives expired.

No. The girls didn't understand. The guys didn't really care. My family would talk about these things, but outside of my home, there was a disconnect that rendered me a complete loner amidst my peers. By this time, Ronnie and I weren't seeing as much of each other, as work and other circumstances had created a rift in our schedules, and I never had another friend quite like him. I didn't pity myself, but I definitely felt the pang of isolation.

Would there be—would there *ever* be—someone for me to fully relate to? To bond with beyond giggles and one-liners? To unite with outside the boundaries of my wily, wink-and-gun exterior? To know the real *me*, and let me see the real *her*?

It's funny sometimes, you know—when the question you're asking is so desperate you've almost given up on finding an answer, and then life (translation: God) presents you with the remedy to your greatest illnesses.

But then again, that's not "funny." It's Divine.

I remember when I met Nita.

Nita was something else…

Her father and sister had just tragically died in a car accident. Nita and her mother had been in the car that night as well, but they had survived. (The cause of the accident, the devastating effect it had on her, and "her side of the story" upon meeting me later on is all detailed in my wife's book, *No Fences: It Started with a Plastic Pony… A Memoir*, released earlier this year.) I had seen Nita around town a few times in a wheelchair, her leg in a cast, and I had thought she was prettier than all the other girls. It didn't matter that I couldn't see how her long legs may have looked in a pair of feminine shorts or how her trim waistline would have complemented a flowy summer dress. It didn't matter to me that her hair was flat, straight, and unstyled as a result of her mobility limitations. The wheelchair didn't phase me a bit. In fact, although she was absolutely stunning from the outside, I would venture to say that it wasn't her looks at all that caught my attention. There was something internal that she radiated unintentionally, something both vulnerably beautiful and innocent that made her an elusive and magnetic mystery.

A mystery I absolutely *had to* solve.

She was an enigma. A gorgeous, striking enigma. I couldn't explain it if I had to. She didn't giggle and flirt and bounce her curls and bat her eyelashes. She didn't have anyone to impress, but *oh* the impression that had on me!

It was an "Ardis to Vida" scenario all over again. The unlikely pair. The odd couple. The unexpected duo. I was smitten from the beginning, and, so help us all, there was no undoing it. Nita didn't appear to return my regard for her, though. I scarcely think she was even aware of me.

She hardly spoke at all, and when she did, it was through clenched teeth, as her mouth had been wired shut to allow her broken jaw to heal following the accident. Half of her face was slack and numb from the damage caused by the accident as well. With all of the trauma she had been through—the internal turmoil that nobody on the outside could fathom and the external maladies that would have caused self-consciousness in social settings—she wasn't taking the lead in any conversation. On the occasion when I did speak to her, she didn't respond to me like the other girls did, which I found challenging. As I observed her while she sat quietly, allowing everyone else to do the talking, I wondered what was going on in that pretty head of hers. Getting to know her was going to be difficult.

Little did I know I would be given another chance to "impress" her.

As fate would have it, a short time later, Dad told me we were going on a "double date" with his girlfriend and her daughter…Nita.

Yes. *The* Nita.

We were going horseback riding. Evidently, the wheelchair and the cast would no longer be a hindrance.

This was my big chance.

When we arrived at the stables, Nita was oblivious to my presence. (And, as she writes in her memoir, this was her first memory of meeting me.) Here I was, the cool cat of Arizona, and all she could think about was the horses. When asked what kind of mount I was looking for, I made sure Nita was in earshot and gave a bombastic response.

"Gimme the fastest one ya got."

The wide-eyed or fascinated expression from a praising Nita never came. She asked for a horse that would be easy to ride, then went about giving her full attention to it when the stable hand brought it out.

I was going to have to try much, *much* harder.

Pulling myself into the saddle of my speedy mount, I glanced over at Nita, who was still drinking in the experience, staring at and stroking her horse as if it had done something more worthy of her attention than I.

"You comin'?" I asked impulsively.

Nita didn't answer me as she pulled herself onto the saddle.

Eager to get on with it, I readied myself to dazzle this girl with my inspiring horseback skills (I had ridden horses in the past, but certainly was not the expert I thought I was) when I saw Dad heading over to talk to us. He regarded Nita as he spoke as well, but it was more than clear that he was directing his warning gaze at me.

"Now, here's the deal, kids," Dad said in a fatherly tone. "You can ride all over the place out here a'far as I care, but whatever you do," he paused at this point, fixed his eyes on mine, and then continued, "*whatever you do…DO NOT* ride up over that hill." Dad pointed to an adjacent, sandy incline.

My back stiffened at the idea of being told what to do—and what NOT to do—by "Daddy" right in front of Nita.

"Why not? It's jist a hill," I said, eyeing Nita to see if my nonchalant, confident reply had wowed her.

It hadn't.

"B'cause," Dad said, "there's a huge mud pit on th' other side of it. If you go near it, your horse an' you both are gonna sink in an' get stuck up to yer breather gills in mud. I don't care where else ya'll go ridin', but that there hill is off limits."

"Okay," Nita said with obedient intention.

"Sure thing," I said casually.

"I *mean* it Joe." Dad cautioned me with a squint.

"Yyyup."

When the embarrassment of being a daddy's boy was over, we were released to the range. What came next was probably the dumbest thing I could have done. As Nita shared from her perspective in her book:

For decades this story has been told and retold within family circles. Each time it is relived, it's equally hard to believe, and it always sounds like some contrived or exaggerated scene from a comedy, but I promise you readers, this is exactly how it happened.

Clarence and Mom went their own way after the warning of the mud pit had been given firmly and irrefutably.

I kid you not…The first thing Joe did, as straight as a bird can fly, was set off in a full gallop toward that hill! Assuming that he planned to eventually go around it, I followed along in the same direction. Watching from behind, I kept expecting him to hug the outskirts of the mud pit…but I was not so fortunate.

Joe didn't first assess the situation, consider his riding skills, and then attempt to show up his father's warnings by dabbling at the edge of danger… No, no, no. That would have been too sensible. Joe, with reckless abandon, straight out of the gate, ran his horse absolutely head-first into that mud pit, as if, with breakneck speed, he was determined to accomplish the most foolhardy, harebrained expression of absurdity he was capable of.

It was quite the performance… (Nita Horn, *No Fences*; Defender Publishing: Crane, MO, 2016; 74)

Sigh. What in the world was I thinking? To this day, I don't even know how to explain my actions. I honestly haven't the foggiest idea what I thought my feat would prove. Even while I was driving that horse toward the mud, I'm sure I must have known that I didn't possess the skills to guide the horse to clear it—nor had I planned to get stuck like I did. So what was I *doing*?!

Way to impress the ladies, Joe.

Nita stumbled out a few words of pure astonishment at my stunt, watched as I sat on the saddle of a horse chest-high in mud and still sinking, and shook her head in understandable bewilderment as I blamed the "stupid horse."

Sliding off the saddle, I trudged through the sludge as Nita went to find Dad and tell him that our outing had ended before it began.

When Dad returned a few minutes later, he was mad as a hornet. I knew he would be, and I had already prepared myself for the tongue-lashing I was about to get. Because of the pure hilarity of the situation as it was observed from Nita's perspective, I will share that part of the narrative from her book. As Nita, her mom, and my dad were coming back around to the pit a minute later, Dad was giving me a well-deserved greeting:

> "Well now, Meathead! Are you happy with your little accomplishment!? Did this little presentation achieve what you hoped it would?"
>
> Joe had nothing to say. Taking his last few steps out of the muck and onto the dry desert sand, he stood quietly and shrugged, probably knowing very well that no explanation or excuse would shine any brighter than his folly at that moment. As Clarence lowered himself from his horse and marched toward the pit, Joe quickly stepped aside to let him pass.
>
> "Tarnation," Clarence went on. "Stupidest thing I ever seen. Just had to go showin' off. Just had to prove somethin'." (Ibid., 76–77)

When told from my own viewpoint of my father's strength, the following event would be anticlimactic. I was used to seeing my dad show his incredible physical force, so this next bit was nothing new to me. Nita, however, had never seen anything like it, and the way she tells of the closing of this day's event is more than just a little amusing:

I glanced at Mom. She was as curious as I was. What on earth did this man [my dad] think he was going to do? Why wasn't he coming up with a plan to remove the horse from the pit? Why wasn't he sending for help?

Trudging directly into and through the miry sludge, Clarence approached the horse, grumbling and hollering intermittently, waving his arms about in a fury. Then wrapping his arms around the horse's torso, he heaved toward the closest drop-off point of the pit.

I was impressed...and judging by her reaction and comments about his strength, so was Mom. I saw a sparkle in her eye as she observed his movements. He actually repositioned that horse a foot's length without the use of any vehicle or machine. He was the vehicle! [That's my dad for you. A total beast.]

I studied the distance between the edge of the pit and Clarence with skepticism. Even if he proved able to pull that horse all the way to the rim of this gluey abyss, he couldn't possibly be planning to extract the horse with his bare hands...

But, as God is my witness, that is exactly what he did.

I remember watching his brute strength with awe. I had never seen a demonstration of such tenacity, such vigor, such brawn! With nothing but his bare hands, Clarence pulled that horse, literally hauling the animal five times his own size, to the shore of the mud. From there, he moved to the horse's side, wrapped his burly limbs under and around the front legs, and lifted! The horse's hooves caught the edge of solid ground, and after a brief struggle, the horse managed to pull himself out completely. Clarence followed shortly behind, covered head to toe in grime and sweat.

And then, as if we hadn't just witnessed an almost inhuman exhibition of strength, Clarence fell straight back into his casual parenting tactics.

"Joe, you've done a lot of stupid things, but that was a doozy. How dumb are you? What's wrong with you? You got somethin' wrong with yer head?"

Still Joe stood without a response. I could tell by his posture and facial expression that he was putting up airs. Despite how embarrassed anyone in his position would have felt, he played it off by his cavalier stance. I'll never forget how Joe looked that day, covered in filth, trying to act unaffected, like a sophisticated teenage stud while his father scolded him right on the spot in front of a girl. [And that was me for you. Always the hip kid.]

"Naw, you ain't got nothin' ta say," Clarence waved his hand dismissively. "Just stand there like a dumb-dumb with your big ridiculous hat [See? Even Dad thought that hat was ridiculous!], thinkin' yer a cowboy. Go on, now! Let's woo the women, shall we? How 'bout we go find ourselves a cliff to jump off, too? Why don't we just get real impressive while we're at it?"

Clarence turned back to his own horse, walking him by the reins toward the stables. Over his shoulder, he continued to mutter.

"Typical kid. Always gotta act like ya know more'n I do about everything. I hope yer happy with that stunt you pulled. Criminy…"

It had been an event for sure, but thanks to Joe and his great descent, the entire joyride lasted five minutes before the rest of our time was spent rescuing horses and cleaning up for the afternoon.

Needless to say, Joe hadn't given off the best first impression. When he ruined my day and deprived me of my dreamy sunshine horseback adventure, I didn't care that he was the cat's meow to all the other girls my age. [And that was Nita for you. Unimpressed by the knight-errant Joe.] Clarence seemed like a nice man who held true promise of happiness and stability for my mother, but there would not be a second "double date." (Ibid., 77–79)

I still laugh out loud when I read how Nita approached this story. *Nobody* knew what I had been trying to do with that horse. Not me, not Dad, not Nita, and evidently not Vidabell, either, as she told Allie and Donna, "Well, I mean, it's your dad! [Everyone in the background of the recording laughs knowingly.] It's just the kind of thing he would do! Maybe to be impressive? Maybe to show he could do it, like some horse whisperer or something?"

No idea.

What I *do* know is that when that day was over, I had gotten Nita's attention alright, but not exactly in the way I had hoped.

When the "double date" came to an end, I went back to my duties at home, taking care of Mom and family and working long hours. Day-to-day life went on as usual, and I found myself more and more often taking to the hills to reflect on my thoughts when I had my fill of counterfeit connection to my peers.

Shortly after the mud incident, Dad and Nita's mother got married.

Vidabell and I drew closer when Dad moved to Oregon with Nita and his new bride, and I visited with her daughter, Lavida, whenever they were around. My sister remembers those days:

> Yeah, your dad has pictures of that. He had long hair and he always wore this floppy hat. [Again with that hat!] He was always proud of [Lavida] because Shannon [Amil's son] was his first nephew, but Lavida was his first niece.... I decided to decorate Lavida's room, and Joe went to the state fair and he won all these stuffed animals. Really cute ones. And he brought them all to Lavida for her first room. And she was just a baby. She had all these stuffed animals in her room and it was really sweet of him. He was always a good uncle.

When Mom passed away a few weeks back, Donna and Allie helped Vidabell organize a few things in her home, and this puppy dog was found amidst boxes of old memories. Mom wasn't there to bring complete certainty, but Vidabell thought there was a good chance this toy was one of the earnings from the state fair I brought home for Lavida.

I'm unendingly grateful for my family during this time. Without Ronnie or another close friend I could share my thoughts with, I began to feel like the odd man out in most areas of life. Despite how readily available my brother, sister, and mother were anytime I needed them, I knew the day would come when that wouldn't be enough. I wanted to settle down someday, regardless of how unlike me that may have seemed to all the girls in my neck of the woods.

Every time I went to see Dad in Oregon, I also got to visit with Nita. I rarely ever saw her, as we were states away, but when we did find ourselves trading pleasantries in passing, she was just as intriguingly transparent—and yet mysterious—as she had been when I had seen her in Arizona. Her guard was always up around me in those early days, but from the beginning, I knew she wasn't happy, either. She was awkward socially, and didn't have any close friends.

Like me.

I mentioned earlier that I saw myself as a real "James Dean of the sands." Nita, also, viewed herself far different than she truly was. Unlike my self-inflation, however, she believed herself to be broken and of little use to the world around her. In her book, she explains:

I was awkward and misunderstood by the majority of the world most of the time. My hair was stringy-straight and "tow-head" blonde, my teeth were crooked because of a cleft palate I had been born with, and I was thin as a rail. Because of the accident, my mouth had been wired shut so my shattered jaw could heal, and for years following, the entire left side of my face was numb and slack. When I opened my mouth to speak or laugh, I looked like someone who had just been shot with novocain, and the effect took years to wear off. Without any feeling in that part of my face, eating was a whole new challenge, and I sometimes found to my horror that I had dribbled on my chin. My speech was slurred, and my confidence in making friends, talking to boys, or participating in group events with people my own age was now all but destroyed. In addition, the crash had turned me into an inverted emotional basket case, generating internal baggage, creating a whole other list of issues in regard to how I related to people from that day forward. The need for a true attachment to others was always present, but never fulfilled. (Nita Horn, *No Fences*; 79–80)

We may have been approaching this adolescent identity crisis from opposing ends—I was the popular one, she was the introverted and shy one—and we may not have had much in common that could be observed by outsiders, but we were *very* similar at heart.

She was alone.

Like me.

After several years as a manager at the Circle One Feedlot, I decided to take a much-needed two-week vacation to go see Dad.

I didn't know at the time that I would never return to live in Arizona.

During that visit, I realized how much I truly had in common with Nita. She felt the connection on her end, too:

[Joe] might have been the cool loner, but he was a loner just the same, and an authentic connection between him and his peers was just as difficult to come by as it had been for me. He was never left wanting for a girlfriend, as the line of interested girls seemingly went on forever. Still, though, nothing between him and the silly girls he had met had ever been genuine.

We were in so many ways polar opposites. The cool kid and the skinny nerd. But when the rubber met the road, we were both terribly lonely and living in a world of strangers. Getting to know Joe from this perspective introduced a bond that shaped both our futures. We were both oddly independent social anomalies where it counted, and because of that, we were perfect for each other. (Ibid., 80)

From my viewpoint, Nita was incredible. I couldn't figure out why she wasn't surrounded by boys, except for the fact that her lack of interest in them was exceedingly apparent. Any person willing to write off her remarkable mind and prodigious intelligence because she had been hurt (physically in the accident or emotionally), or simply because she wasn't the openly flirtatious or giggly fish dominating the sea at that age, was losing out on the opportunity to gain the companionship of a priceless and treasured jewel. Not only was she gorgeous on the outside, but I didn't have to bond with her for long to learn that her core ran deep.

We could talk about lots of things—things people our age didn't appear interested in. When I mentioned some of the thoughts that I obsessed over regarding the universe or God or life or the future, her feedback came like well-seasoned meat to a starving canine. How *refreshing* Nita's brain was to me!

And her inability to be fake or contrived simply made me fall in love with her over and over again. I didn't feel like I was talking to a mask. She may have held back a little in her interaction with me (and who wouldn't: "James Dean of the sands" in the "stupid hat"), but what sides of her she allowed me to see were of a real person. There was a real person inside her! An innocent one. A sweet one.

A lonely one.

Like me.

Like Ardis with Vida, I couldn't help myself. She was from another world, one completely foreign to my own, but she wasn't the "broken" individual she thought she was, and I was determined to prove that to her.

My dad was now married to her mom, so for what felt like the longest era of my life, we would not allow ourselves to have a relationship beyond friendship. Over time, however, when it was clear that was what felt most natural, we addressed the elephant in the room.

First, I had never lived with Nita. I had been over a thousand miles away living with my mother in Arizona. I had never occupied the same space as Nita in any living conditions, so nothing about our association had ever been brotherly or sisterly. I was just "that kid" who came around once in a while, and Nita was just "that girl" who lived at the house I rarely dropped by to visit. Second, there was absolutely no blood relation between us. Third, we were able to acknowledge that if my dad and her mom had not signed a marriage license, Nita and I likely would have instinctively formed a relationship based on our own chemistry anyway. Just because our parents had connected didn't mean we weren't allowed to. And fourth, we were both so painfully hungry for a legitimate bond—a compatible bond—with other human life, that when it arrived between Nita and me, we were able to recognize a once-in-a-lifetime friendship and union opportunity for what it was.

Once we talked it through, we concluded it was permissible to see where a relationship would go.

From that point forward, my trips out to the corners of the world to reflect had a completely different and amazing feel now that she was beside me.

Vidabell remembers: "I never met a girlfriend [of Joe's]. I never did personally, *ever*, until your mother. The only girlfriend I ever met was your mom.... He just fell in love with her. They were very young. It was like wow!... I don't think he truly cared about any of his other little girlfriends that he might have had, but Nita was the only girlfriend I ever met, and he was crazy about her."

The desires of my heart were planted in Nita. I didn't even know at the time what "desires of the heart" even meant, nor did I think prior to meeting Nita that fulfillment would ever be found in a woman. It was as if some grand Creator of the universe knew me better than I knew myself, saw my needs, and invested in my happiness. It was as if something or Someone above those Arizona stars saw my potential and provided for me despite my juvenile arrogance. The more I got to know Nita, the more I loved her. The more vulnerability she showed me, the more I wanted to protect her. The more we shared our thoughts about the future, the more I wanted her to be in it.

I had at that point determined that, one day, her presence beside me *would* be "to have and to hold, 'til death do us part." It just had to be that way. I had to have her as a companion for life, and I was willing to give up anything for that to happen.

I may not have been a believer in the sincerest sense by that time, but I do believe that the Spirit had a hold on me. And it may not have been within a church or Bible study, but out in the desert, God knew that in my own way, I was seeking Him. Far too many circumstances of my life were headed down a path of serious trouble just before I met Nita. Arrested for being an accessory to car theft, setting fire to buildings by my own unlawful interpretations of justice, sneaking around the cities after dark, generally acting like a punk any time I could get away with it, flirting a little too often with girls who had let me know they had the time and place if I had the interest, and simply all the avenues I was seeking to find a thrill.

I never became an inordinately destructive member of society, because God guided my path to the store for a Coke and peanuts to meet Ronnie, an innocent soul and interference from so much worse I might have done.

I never became a cold-hearted womanizer, because God brought me Nita, my manna in the wilderness.

I never became "Joe the criminal," because God graciously steered me in a different direction, blinded me to myself, and gave me eyes to see the wonders of the universe that science can't explain: my encounter on the road to Damascus.

Did I, Thomas "Joe" Horn, take Nita to be my lawfully wedded wife?

I did. I would again. I still do.

I do every day.

That woman is the reason I live, the air I breathe, and the driving force behind every decision I make, second only to God, Himself.

We have been married now for over forty years, and it has been clear every hour since the day we met that even when I didn't know what I was doing, wandering around like a cocky punk and drawing ever nearer to a path of destruction, God was preparing my *purpose*. A footprint, written and formed since before the doctors ever told my mother to abort me.

And Nita was a new beginning.

If it weren't for her, I would have likely continued to feed the mundane circumstances with my life through thrills and joyrides. If it weren't for her, I probably would have flirted and flattered my way into an unfulfilling relationship. If it weren't for her, nobody would have witnessed my death in the middle of the night years ago and stood beside me to confirm the experience was real.

If it weren't for her, I may never have truly found God.

If it weren't for *God*, I wouldn't have found Nita.

God provides. He provided daily bread for Ardis and Vida at Mac's Trading Post. He provided strength for Mom during pregnancy. He provided wisdom for Dr. Shackleford when he attended to my head injuries after the accident.

He provided Nita when I didn't know what I was looking for.

And He will provide for you. Whatever your needs are, when you closest to giving up, He will bring you the strength, wisdom, and people you need to continue in the development of your footprint.

As for *how* I came to genuinely know God—and the strange, nearly unexplainable details that parallel that turn in my life—turn the page.

Me at around 18 years old playing my future mother-in-law Wanda's guitar. She is the one who taught me how to play, beginning with "Wildwood Flower."

Me around 17 years old with Dad. Check out that cool hair!

Four

The Boy Who Finally *Was* "As Good As Gone"

When Nita and I married, it was without a big spectacle. Neither she nor I had any important friends who needed to witness an elaborate exchange of vows, and our family hadn't expressed any specific hopes of us having a glorious, ribbon-adorned ceremony. Nita had lost her little sister, who would have been her maid of honor, in the car accident, and she had also lost her father, who would have given her away—so putting on airs at a big party didn't seem to matter to her like it may have to many other young girls. I didn't have two nickels to rub together, and had been giving nearly all my money to Mom, so when I popped the question to Nita, the "ring" I had obtained was the pull-tab mechanism from a soda can. In those days, the tin ring was much larger and was designed to pull completely off the can, so I wiggled off the tab and slipped it on her finger.

She said yes.

To the cool cat. To the closet loner. To the James Dean of the sands.

When we walked down to the local courthouse and paid the ten dollars required for a marriage license, we were both committed as much as two young kids could be, but we had no idea of what the life ahead of us looked like. We had agreed to marry even before we had any clue about where we would live.

As my dad had become increasingly aware of Nita's passion about horses, he made it his personal side job to scout the local listings for budget horses while I had been living in Arizona with Mom. At one point, he took Nita out to see a horse named "Shorty," which was for sale at a hundred dollars even. He was a sad-looking horse, full of worms, caked in mud, and overpriced. However, because Dad and Nita had been looking for a horse for some time, when they finally found one in their price range, they bought it.

Dad taught Nita how to care for the horse, and Nita walked down to the berry fields almost every day to pick berries to earn a meager allowance to pay for Shorty's riding equipment. During this time, Nita grew close to Shorty and began to see him as more than just a pet. Because she hadn't bonded with *people*, he was a friend with whom she shared her secrets and woes.

Before long, through more thrifty scouting, Dad and Nita found another horse to bring home: "Little One."

Shorty and Little One. Nita had two friends now. They meant the world to her, and she spent every waking moment with them when she wasn't at school or picking berries. the two horses all but entirely replaced Nita's need for camaraderie amongst her peers. Each meant a great deal more to her than just domesticated animals living in a barn outside, and for several years while I lived in Arizona, Nita poured herself—heart and soul—into caring for her most precious buddies.

When I asked Nita to marry me a few years later, willing to leave Arizona behind and begin things anew with her, we didn't have a place to live or any money to invest in our future together. I had been taking every job I could get. For a while I worked as a framer for three different construction companies, and after sending money to Mom and paying for the necessities of life, I couldn't seem to save enough even for a down payment on a starter apartment. Nita and I agreed I needed help getting some funds together—*but*—we also agreed that we were grown-ups now; therefore, we refused to ask for money from our parents. If we were going to get married and be adults, we had to act like adults, beginning with whatever meager launch we could scrape together on our own.

The help came from the sale of Shorty and Little One.

Of course Nita hated having to sell her two best friends. It broke her heart to abandon these two four-legged family members. The sorrowful goodbye felt premature and unfair, gouging the stability of all things familiar to a young woman who had so recently lost her father and sister. In addition, however, Nita knew that she couldn't keep the horses, even if we had the money for a rental, because we wouldn't have a place to keep them if we lived in an apartment. That was the only consolation she took with her to the auction house the day she stroked their manes for the last time and imparted upon them her farewell secrets.

Together, the pair sold in a lot for ninety dollars. They went to the same home, to a family that promised to love and care for them, so Nita was able to release them in trade for a down payment on our future. With the proceeds from the sale, I filled the gas tank, bought a month's worth of groceries, and rented a small house. (Nita's account about these horses and this era of our early marriage is spread over an entire chapter of her own book, *No Fences*.)

The hit-and-miss construction jobs helped, but I knew I had to find something unwavering, so I found a job that would at least promise a steady workload for the season. A local farmer by the name of Gene Stockhoff was hiring a field hand to help harvest of vegetables. I met him, introduced myself as "Tom" (my real name, by which I would now be known in our new life in Oregon), promised to work hard, and landed the position. I had been taught to work hard even in the Arizona heat, so when I took this job in the fields of Oregon, I didn't fear sweat, manual labor, or getting my hands dirty. I knew you couldn't earn money by standing around, and now I had a wife to think about. If I had ever "piddled around," as my sister remembers (thanks, Vidabell…), I was definitely past that now. The work ethics instilled by Mom and Dad were showing their true colors, and I was toiling away in those fields like my life depended on it—and in a way, it was, since no money meant no food on the table for Nita and me.

Nita helped out with odd jobs she could find for her hands to do, but we hadn't been married long before the symptoms that she was expecting a little one required her to take it easy. I paid very close attention to her condition at the time, since pregnancy had posed such a risk for my mother. I wasn't the pregnant one, and I was the man of my new little house, so Nita needed to to spend most of her time caring for herself—and her belly—as far as I was concerned.

Boy did she keep a clean house, though. And she tended to every one of my needs. She was not idle.

Soon after the job with Gene started, he informed me that he was more than just satisfied with my work. My determination to harvest the best crops was transparent, sure…but he also started to notice something about my character that many acquaintances of mine had not yet seen. Instead of merely observing my "punk" side, Gene perceived a young newlywed striving to make the best life he could and search for truth. I have no idea—and will never have any educated guess—as to *why* Gene saw potential in me as any long-term investment. Nonetheless, he made an exceptional offer to help Nita and me get a better start in life.

He said he would clear an acre of his own land, install a septic tank, dig a well, pave a driveway, route electricity from the road, co-sign as guarantor on a loan for a mobile home purchase, and place the home right there on his property. He would pay for *everything*, except the mobile home (which, by extension, was coming from him anyway, since my income was through the job he had given me). When the offer seemed too good to be true, he upped the ante, informing me that he wouldn't even charge us rent!

I still have a hard time understanding his generosity. That man not only sacrificed his own land and funds for us, he placed himself in the vulnerable position of trusting two almost-strangers. If Nita and I had any hidden or malicious intent, we could have hosted wild parties, dealt drugs, trashed his land, abused our new house, and left him responsible for the mortgage on a useless mobile home. We certainly *seemed* like nice kids, but people aren't always what they seem. How could he possibly have known that we would make good on the promise to accept such an offer gratefully and respectfully?

Floored by his proposal, Nita and I accepted with more "thank yous" on our lips than I will ever be able to count. Construction began immediately, and within only a couple months of the agreement, we were moving into a home we now owned on a land we didn't owe a penny on, with working electricity and plumbing.

My best guess in explaining such an extraordinary deal would be that God had placed a peace in Gene's heart about that decision; God knew we needed help; He must have told Gene he would be the vessel through which He would minister to us and we would not take such an investment in vain.

And we didn't.

From that moment on, Nita and I took very special care of everything that had been entrusted to us.

A perk that we hadn't discussed in the original deal was the inheritance that came with the land and home: a resident mentor. Our landlord was a good man, and he knew a lot about life and the mysteries in it that I hadn't been able to figure out on my own out there under the Arizona sun.

Gene was a Christian, and like other Christians, he believed that God had created the world and all the people in it.

That included me.

If what Gene said was true, I was no longer a random happenstance of science, and my life had a purpose beyond this temporal reality. Better yet, Gene said, a Spirit was available to guide people toward achieving their potential purpose. And the price I had to pay to invite this Guiding Light into my life?

Believing in the Son of God as Savior of humankind. Believing that He came, died, and rose again—and that His power is alive on earth.

Other than that, Gene said, the presence of that Guiding Light was *free*.

Of course, I had known this much from what my mother told me, but as no prophet is accepted in his own hometown (Luke 4:24), the greatest wisdom is not always learned from one's own parents at home, even when those parents have the greatest wisdom. Hearing someone other than Mom present the secrets of the universe in similar ways confirmed that thoughts of God and a Powerful Being above that sky somewhere were not as crazy as they had appeared to be in my past.

Nevertheless, I analyzed myself into a state of near spiritual-growth paralysis as I continued to give every *other* explanation for the unseen realm around us a fair chance. The supernatural, to me, was too great a mystery to merely wash it all away in a quick, Sunday-school summation. I was too resistant to a "simple" Gospel that gave everyone on earth the same access to the eternal gift of salvation just because they professed belief in a Man who came to die thousands of years ago on a cross outside Jerusalem. It was a pretty story, and something about hearing it inspired me, but I was determined to find the truth to the mysteries of the universe on my own.

I was Thomas Horn. *I* would prove to be more capable where others had failed to determine what all of this meant.

As it turns out, *I* was just Doubting Thomas, who had to experience contact with the nail-scarred hands in my own way to believe Jesus Christ was who He said He was. And when I did, it changed me forever…

Although I was absolutely smitten with Nita from the beginning of our relationship, once we were married, a tension started to brew. I was never cruel to her, I never set out to hurt her (emotionally or physically), but I was a goon at times. I did love her. I always loved her. Yet, I found a funny way of showing it as I criticized a lot of the things she did around the house and made her feel less than desirable. I also began to retreat from her, just like I had done with my friends in Arizona. After a long day's work, I would find some excuse to go off into the bedroom alone and reflect. There was an enormous hole in my life somewhere, and I wasn't going to be happy until it was filled with a greater perception of the unknown.

Night after night, I poured myself into ruminating over the paranormal, extrasensory perception, and the mystical domain. Things like telepathy, clairvoyance, precognition, retrocognition, and parapsychology had too much attention in the secular world to simply leave all of one's potential to God, Satan, angels, demons, and all other beings governed by them. I started to believe that mankind had a layer of independent power apart from external sources, including God, if we could only discover the pathways to tap into it. As a result, my evenings were increasingly absorbed with like-minded contemplations. (Note: Years later, when *The 700 Club* featured my testimony on their show, the producers had me dramatize these evenings by sitting in an eerie, brown bathrobe in front of lit candles at the mirror with my hands in a "prayer" position and my eyes closed. Today, that dramatization would be received differently than it was in the 1980s, thanks to the "Satanic Panic" era that immediately followed that episode. To the audience of the day, it was only insinuated that I was meditating. In order to completely strike from the record the notion that I was ever "praying" to something spiritually dark, I would like to make the point very clear that I was not intentionally inviting anything shady or satanic into my life or into my heart. I was just searching for truth, and that's a hard thing to pair with visual imagery that tells a story, so they were doing the best they could with the skills they had. In order for their audience to take my testimony seriously, they had to assign serious dramatization as a parallel, and a casual guy sacked out on his bed "thinking thoughts" wouldn't have achieved that.)

I immersed myself, almost to obsessive magnitudes, in believing that mankind did not need to submit to God or Jesus Christ to transcend to a higher awareness of being. The Gospel may have explained what one Man did two thousand years ago, but what proof did the Gospel have that this Man had any true power as the literal Son of God, and how did that relate to the potential a person would have while experiencing life on this planet? For that matter, how could any of those accounts by Matthew, Mark, Luke, John, Paul, or any other New Testament author be proven true? Historical record from extrabiblical sources most definitely supported that Jesus was born, lived, ministered with supernatural abilities, and was crucified, but did that also mean that He was the Son of God? Was he messianic just because those writers said so? Did it mean that, as churchgoers and Gene said, Jesus Christ's very name—*just His name alone*—had great authority?

It wasn't that I scoffed at the notion of Jesus Christ. Nor did I directly regard God irreverently. But I didn't *seek Him*, either. Even before my beliefs about God and Christ were nailed down, I believed in the existence of evil (as I shared with *The 700 Club* during the interview), and I didn't want to be evil—or unite with evil in order to become enlightened—but I sought to find answers to the void I felt through my own means. That left little room for Christ to intervene in my life. With Christ and the Father shoved aside while I tormented myself with unending questions and picked on Nita in my unhappiness, a gate was left open wide for intervention of another kind.

My long-term memory may have been damaged as a child, but there are some things I believe God will never let me forget. That night in that mobile home—when *something* outside the confines of our perceivable universe appeared to me—is one such memory.

I was in bed staring at the ceiling with my fingers laced behind my head, and Nita was asleep beside me. I was, once again, lying awake pondering the powers of the human mind and extrasensory perception. I allowed my thoughts to wander into the farthest reaches of the supernatural I could comprehend, and I was not afraid as I imagined myself achieving a transcendental control over my earthly life through the total surrender of my consciousness to a greater sixth sense.

And then…I sensed something…

A pressure came into the room slowly, seeping in from the walls and the ceiling. The whole room was gradually pervading to its brim with a presence. This thing, this being, may have been trying to entice me with its force and initiate me into a communion with darkness, and there is *no doubt in my mind* that if my mom and dad hadn't instilled a deep caution within me and the innate ability to recognize evil for what it is— *and* if God hadn't been watching over me—I might have been fooled into thinking this was the moment I had tapped into: that "higher level" I had been searching for so intensely.

However, I did identify the evil for what *it* was, and despite its attempted seduction toward the part of me that wished to become something more than *I* was, I knew it ultimately had wicked intentions.

I was only barely aware that Nita had awakened. Until this point, I had not uttered a word or made any sound, and Nita had only moments before been sound asleep. It was the manifestation of something sinister, in and of itself, that jolted her from an otherwise restful slumber.

It was a spiritual suffocation. My body was breathing normally, but the darkness was pressing in on me to the point that my very essence— my internal core—was asphyxiating. Whereas I had been the king cobra of bravery at the very edge of dabbling minutes prior, now a fear like nothing I had ever felt before bubbled up from my gut. I glanced at Nita, who was visibly scared out of her mind as she clinched a blanket up to her chin. Our eyes could not see anything out of the ordinary. We looked at each other and around the room, and it looked just as our bedroom always did. There was no maniacal laughter, no green smoke, no smell or taste in the air, and nothing reached out to touch our skin.

Yet somehow, strangely, all senses even in our physiological makeup were being affected by this malicious energy. I felt it…forcing itself beyond any safety nets like a deep sea predator you can't see or touch or smell or feel, but whose nearby existence is setting off every red-alert detection alarm within the mind.

Waiting.

Drawing closer.

Swarming in from every direction.

Preparing to either invite us to join it, or devour us whole.

From somewhere within me, a sudden Truth dawned upon my cognition and dominated my thoughts. A Truth that I recognized as familiar. One that had been locked away and refused, but the power behind which I immediately trusted. Something that I knew innately. I didn't know where it came from, but in one overwhelmingly powerful moment, I was at once aware that it was by only one Name that we would be delivered from malevolence and danger.

I didn't bow my head or get on my knees. I didn't stand up and lift my hands to the air. I didn't take hold of Nita's hand and join her in that "where two or more are gathered" agreement. I clutched on to whatever fabrics on that bed my hands could grasp and opened my lips to call for help from the Divine like a petrified child.

"Jesus… Jesus… Jesus…"

Over and over.

"Jesus… Jesus… Jesus…"

Again and again.

"Jesus… Jesus… Jesus…"

I wasn't shouting, but I didn't need to; it wasn't the volume of my voice that invoked unearthly intervention. I wasn't speaking with authority, because I didn't know how; it wasn't my own influence that called forth from the sky the Power from whom all demons flee. I wasn't shaking my fists, boisterously rebuking, or railing against the fires of hell, but Someone knew more than I did about the warfare that was going on in that room; it wasn't from my own strength that the Creator—who makes Satan tremble and principalities crumble—descended upon our home.

As I continued to repeat the Name of Jesus, a feeling of safety augmented around Nita and me. As the manifestation of holiness emerged, it pushed away the evil. If I could have seen into the spiritual realm at that moment, I'm positive I would have witnessed the very walls of that mobile home bend outward and threaten to break by the presence of God. I'm sure I would have heard the screams of that thing's craven exit as it yielded our fates to the utmost sovereign Ruler. (Here, too, *The 700 Club* used special effects imagery that was symbolically proficient in telling a story, but was not entirely accurate as far as what each of us experienced that night. Through dramatization, the broadcast showed a visible being hovering over our beds, cackling and waving its hands around in a cloud of green light. When I started saying the Name of Jesus in the dramatization, the evil thing shrieked and left as the room cleared. As stated in the previous pages, the being was absolutely present, but it was invisible. Yet, that was television in the 1980s for ya...)

There is no describing the relief. When you live day to day without that brand of fear, and then it comes upon you suddenly, it's easy to take for granted what "normal" feels like the rest of the time. But from this one reliance upon Christ, having beheld with my own senses something powerfully vile retreating from my bedroom like a coward just because one word—one *Name*—was uttered, my search for transcendence through the power of self ended.

My standard of treatment toward Nita was rectified after this episode. Instead of finding something to be annoyed about, I found myself once again adoring every move she made and wishing to prove that to her in every interaction.

I returned to the fields the next day. Life carried on as usual, but I was holding a grander interest in God, and Gene was the helpful recipient of many questions. He and I talked most about the vegetable harvest, but when the shop talk was over, I no longer hesitated to pick his brain on matters of a higher importance.

Little did I know that while Gene was mentoring me between loads of corn, green beans, and carrots, God was working on Nita back in the mobile home...

Our first child was born while we lived on Gene's land, and we named her Althia—although, when she was old enough to make her preferences known, she asked to be called Allie, and we have done so ever since. Having a child really does, as they say, change the way a person looks at life. I cared about Allie and wanted to instill within her not only the ability to discern right from wrong as it applies to this life, but also any truths relating to what follows this life. Nita also felt this weight of sudden parenthood, and as she tended to the baby and kept the house clean like the true Suzie Homemaker she was, she allowed Christian television and radio channels to play in the background, because she was just as curious about this God as I was.

Neither Nita nor I was saved at this point, but that episode in the bedroom affected us, and we were both constantly needled by an urgency to figure out what all this talk of "eternal salvation" really meant. Odd, though...we never really talked about the subject to each other. I assumed that Nita had pretty much forgotten the event, and she had assumed the same about me. Not that we would have forgotten that it happened, but that we would have set aside its significance, chalking it up to something bizarre that we would have the rest of our lives to sort out. Having never really followed up with one another about how the radically supernatural occurrence made us feel, all thoughts that pressed us throughout the day regarding God were isolated to each of us independently from the other. (Without a doubt, the Holy Spirit was working on both of us at the same time, despite our lack of discussion it.)

Day after day, Nita played with Allie, read to her, talked to her about how to fold laundry (well before she could understand a word), nursed minor boo-boos, kissed scraped knees, and loved on her as if she had taken motherhood classes for years prior to giving birth. Allie grew to be an adorable toddler, frolicking in dresses and role-playing elaborate games with Nita involving communication skills far beyond her age. The two gave me a happy place to come home to at the end of every hard work day, and my heart swelled for both of them increasingly.

And life went on this way for about two years.

One day, just after Allie's second birthday, I was at work when Nita was doing dishes. She heard a voice from the television screen:

"You folks at home can ask Jesus into your heart also."

Nita's ears perked. She walked away from the kitchen sink and stood in the living room to hear what this minister was saying. It was Billy Graham. She had heard him a lot lately, and of all the televangelists whose ministries had reached the mobile home through the awesome witnessing tool the television had become, his had continued to prickle her intellect—no, her *heart*—more than all the rest. The way he spoke of the power of God and the love of Christ had planted a longing within her to believe.

"Committing your life to Christ is not limited to a building or an event. Just get on your knees, now, here, *today*, right where you are, and ask."

Nita had become exhausted from all the thoughts swarming about in her head for the previous two years. She had felt for what seemed like an eternity already that she really did, deep down, believe in Christ— and it was only a matter of admitting to herself that she was ready to commit to her faith by accepting Christ and then living for Him.

Right there, with an apron tied around her waist and a dishrag in her hand, she knew the time had arrived. And Billy Graham's very next words offered direct confirmation of that fact.

"Invite Him in. Do it now."

It was time.

Nita got on her knees in front of the television and listened further while the televangelist spoke of something called the "sinner's prayer." As he led the prayer, Nita repeated his words. When she finished, there was no light pouring through the ceiling above the TV, no angels singing, and no triumphant trumpet blasts. She had given her heart to the Lord, and she had meant it, but it was without the emotions or hyped circumstances that can, at times, lead new converts to later question the sincerity of their initial decision. At this moment, Nita merely stood to her feet and thought, *Well, that's done. I guess God must be happy with me now.*

She had not been taught any kind of theology, therefore didn't know that although nothing changed in her living room following her decision, in the spiritual upstairs, legions of angels were celebrating what would become her lifetime commitment to Christ. But not more than a few days would pass before Nita would see the first God-inspired consequence of her new communion with the Divine.

The next item on the list she had to consider was *me.*

Her commitment had given her a sense of relief, knowing that at least for the time being, she had done all she felt was required to please the Lord. On the other hand, she felt a mild undertone of trepidation, considering her know-it-all husband "didn't need" God (or so she had assumed, based on all my previous dabbling in self-empowerment), and therefore might not approve of her placing God first. Additionally, there was the notion that making a decision for Christ should be followed by a certain level of deeper understanding, and that required attendance at a church or Bible study—neither of which I had given any sign of being interested in.

Days after Billy Graham led Nita through the sinner's prayer over the television, she was once again at the sink, washing dishes. Her prayer was not polished, her tone never changed, and she didn't follow any pious rules handed to her from a minister—but God heard her just the same:

"God, I don't know what to do right now. I do believe in you, but I cannot force Tom to believe in you or accept that I do. There's no way around it. I need you to deal with Tom. Amen."

It may not have been an earth-shattering, fiery, "claim it in the name of God" prayer, but while Nita was saying these simple words at home about a man she thought was immovably opposed to religion of any kind, I was at work...and it was then that I decided the timing was right for us to plug in to a local body of believers. I came home, walked straight into the kitchen, didn't even say hello or greet anyone, and casually asked Nita what her thoughts were about attending a church. She was stunned by the timing of my words. Just a few hours earlier in the day, she had prayed that God would deal with me, and now *this*.

Her faith was strengthened: Evidence showed that God *does* hear even the simplest of prayers and from the simplest of individuals.

The following Sunday, we headed to a church in Amity, Oregon. We had no idea of what to expect once we arrived, but we were guarded nonetheless, as we both had ingrained expectations of "hellfire and brimstone" folk residing in places such as these. Sharks, waiting to taste blood in the water and attack the weakest among them for their own gain. The concept of judgment within a church building had not been lost on Nita or myself.

What we found there was precisely the opposite of what we feared, and it was exactly what we needed. Thank God for that, because had we been greeted with disdain for our appearance or having been a little rough around the edges with no formal training on how to behave in a church setting (as so many have been before and after us), we may have said phooey on the whole deal and fallen back into old patterns of behavior or thought. Yet, the church, as small the congregation was, was packed with loving mentors. Each person was as interested in us as the next: They wanted to know where we came from, what we did for a living, what our interests were, whether Nita liked to cook, whether I liked to play golf, and generally who we were as people. I was a little taken aback, because I knew that sincere Christians would care about our belief system and eternal fate, but I didn't realize they would care about us as individuals before they knew whether we were saved.

These people nurtured and discipled Nita and me, caring and loving the *people* they were talking to, and never pressuring us beyond comfort to take in too much too fast about this Christ fellow we didn't really know very well. They were all immediately friends first, and that opened our ears to hear what else they would share with us regarding their long-tempered faith in God and Christ resurrected.

I remember the Fullers, the Osbands, the Holtz family, Sister Morrow, and Wyoming Rosebud Dollar in particular. The Fullers became what Nita and I called our "spiritual parents"—in no way a replacement of our earthly and biological parents, but as motherly and fatherly figures in our infant walk with God. (To this day, all three of my children refer to them as "Grandma and Grandpa Fuller.") These families invited us into their homes and lives, adopting us as one would an orphan, tending to all our needs both earthly and infinite. On rare occasions, they would visit us at our home, and never once did they flinch at the secular-looking items we had. (One such item was a painting that depicted dark forces swirling around on a velvet canvas; we removed the painting soon after we both devoted ourselves to Christ, but prior to that moment, it was seen by some of our church friends.) When social gatherings took place at the church, we were welcomed with open arms.

Nita joined a quilters club, where the women would get together and hand-stitch blankets—both to donate to the needy as well as to enjoy a simple hobby. While there, the age-old quilting and needlework skills were passed from one generation to another, and soon Nita was making blankets of her own. As she quickly discovered, however, the club of blanket-stitchers hadn't merely been established for the purpose of sewing. Casual conversations about parenting, God, and family values were inevitably brought up during the quilting sessions, giving Nita great insight on motherhood and marriage—without ever having being directly called aside and talked to with a waggling of a finger. When she had questions about God or theology, she felt free to ask without feeling like all eyes were on her, since the ladies were all there to visit, not to proselytize. (Sadly, many of these wonderful and innovative mentoring clubs are gone from the church, having been replaced with more formal, categorical Bible study groups. Whereas today's groups most definitely *do* have an immense value to young believers, and many would feel lost without such study groups, the social atmosphere of yesteryear's clubs and circles were frequently less intimidating to new believers. Additionally, they provided an environment of spontaneous chatter, which led to friendship, which bred a kind of mentorship that lasted. If new believers today felt they had a friendship with someone beyond the boundaries of *just* what the Bible says, they might find themselves later having more ties back to the faith when the hype of their conversion has waned or when tension within the church body drives them away. Alas, I am sad that these kinds of mentorship groups are nearly but a memory in this country.)

I found many ways of connecting to the men in social settings, and their approach to this simple "anyone can be saved no matter who they were before" Gospel ministered to me deeply in ways that I would take with me for the rest of my life.

I wish there were more people like the Fullers, the Osbands, the Holtz family, Sister Morrow, and Wyoming Rosebud Dollar today.

Needless to say, I gave my heart to the Lord alongside Nita, and together, we began slowly plucking from our hearts and home the things that distracted us from God's true purpose for us, whatever that was.

At home, we began to pray and read the Bible together, which brought us closer than we had ever been. Whenever we ran across a passage in Scripture that we didn't understand, we had multiple resources to reflect upon the verses with, which only strengthened our faith when we came together again with answers. Little Allie was enjoying church as well, and enjoyed a lot of doting attention upon her every Sunday when she walked through the doors wearing a frilly dress or earned a gold star on a scribbly Sunday school coloring paper.

We were a different family than we had been just months prior, and I was feeling really good about the direction we were heading when the next supernatural event occurred.

One night after going to bed next to Nita, I drifted off to sleep, and at some point in the middle of the night, my consciousness was jerked to a place I had never seen. I couldn't comprehend its brilliance. Contemplating my surroundings, I wondered where I was, where I had come from, how long I had been here, and why I had no memories of getting here...wherever *here* was.

At that moment, I knew this was no dream; it was too vivid to be anything less than real. In fact, it felt *realer* than any previous reality I had known. Had I died?

Yes, I had.

I barely became aware of this supernatural backdrop when I abruptly found myself standing somewhere before a spectacular pillar of light (*or was it a throne?*). It was so bright, so intense and penetrating—glistening with vibrant streams of silver and blue and gold emanating the most unexplainable, yet awe-inspiring presence—that I could hardly keep my eyes open or my face toward the radiance.

And I was urgently exclaiming something I couldn't possibly understand: "Please, Lord, don't let me forget. Please don't let me forget! IT'S TOO WONDERFUL!"

How much time had I spent in this surreal place? What had I just observed that so profoundly influenced my desire to remember it? And what was it I was even talking about? Why was I so desperate to recall something I had obviously feared forgetting? And how had I known I was standing before the LORD?

Suspended there like a marionette hanging on wires, I was somehow aware that "memories" from only moments before stood just beyond my ability to summon back into my conscious mind again. (But were "moments" or "time" even factors in this place?) Whatever had been revealed to me was already gone, leaving a hungry void in the place of a great revelation.

But I *had* known something...of that I was sure. A disclosure of vast importance had dawned within my cognition like a great, vibrating bell, alerting the depths of my very soul to a certainty that trumped any knowledge I've ever held in my finite brain…and it had come through no invitation of my own. It hadn't been *my* idea. That much was clear. It had been a truth that electrified my deepest consciousness…something about *the future*. The data was there. I had visualized it, I had *seen* it, and then it had been blocked from my access again; I had been told I would not remember the details.

But why? What would be the purpose in that?

Something else had happened, too. Somehow, I knew that a scroll of some kind had unrolled before me depicting scenes of a distant tomorrow, a hereafter, a time ahead—*my* time ahead—playing out on what looked like silvery parchment. The image of this was as clear and as believable as if I were watching a movie, with rich depictions of a destiny or possible future where something extraordinary and miraculous was taking place. A cinematic conveyance of a personal fate. A "potential existence" that had been downloaded into my subconscious mind—or *soul*. Then, for some reason, it departed my intellect as quickly as it had appeared.

Had a revelation of some type been sealed within me, perhaps something intended for a later time?

My thoughts raced, and I started to repeat, "Lord, please, don't let me forget," but I stopped short as, just then, a deep, still, small voice countered, "You will not remember…and it is time for you to go back now."

I heard a thunder clap and found myself falling backward, gliding rapidly, as if I had been dropped out of an airplane window or was let loose by some heavenly hands that had been holding me above, my arms and legs gliding up and down now against a cloudless sky.

As I fell, I gazed unblinkingly upward in amazement. The brilliance, which had just been in front of me, was moving swiftly away into the distance, and yet I wasn't afraid. A high-pitched whistling sound began rushing in around my ears, and I thought it must be the sound of the air carrying me aloft as I plummeted toward the earth. A moment later, I observed the oddest thing: The roof of my house literally enveloped me as I passed effortlessly through it, and then it felt as if I had landed on my bedroom mattress with a thud…

I sat straight up, took a desperate, shuddering, deep inhalation, and then slowly let the breath out as I realized that something extraordinary had occurred. Wherever I had been, whatever I had seen, now I was back to the "real" world, and this material, earthly substance all around me straightaway felt far less authentic than the other place I had been. It was like *this* cosmos, *this* dimension, *this* realm that everyone calls "life" was merely a temporal and trivial matrix of existence that I was now being required to return to after tasting the marvelous phenomenon of a genuine, superior domain.

It was the middle of the night and I sat there for a few seconds, possibly in shock, trying to determine what had happened.

I could feel my chest burning…and then I heard something.

Sobbing. Right next to me. As the tears flowed, my young wife had her head bowed, resting on her hands.

Once my eyes adjusted to the darkness, I found Nita's isolated stare. She looked as if she had been crying desperately, and she had an unfamiliar expression conveying what I somehow already understood: We had both gone through an experience far more irregular than anything we ever could have prepared for.

"Nita," I said softly, "what's going on? Why are you crying?"

It took a while for her to collect herself, but once she did, she tearfully described how she had awakened to find me dead. I had no pulse, no breath, no heartbeat, and my skin was cold to the touch—and not just for a few seconds. I had remained in that condition for approximately fifteen minutes, she estimated, while she had screamed for me to wake up, pounded on my chest, and attempted something like CPR. My face was contorted in wild expression. My hands were crumpled up next to my head, fingers partly curled inward on themselves like a man creeping up on someone in a classic "boo" scare. My skin was ashen, and my muscles were stiff as a board.

I had been absolutely, beyond a doubt, dead.

I had been, for the *third* time in my life, "as good as gone."

We didn't have a phone in those days, and because it was somewhere around midnight, Nita had been unsure of what to do. She told me she had been about to try pulling me outside to the car to take me to the hospital when I had jerked up, taken a deep breath, and looked at her.

No matter how incredible this narrative seems, it really did happen to me a long time ago. Later, and since then, I understood why God had allowed my wife to wake up and find me in that condition. Without her eyewitness account that night, uncertainties about the supernaturalism of the experience would have undoubtedly crept into my mind over the years. That I had been dead for a significant period of time—not breathing and therefore not taking in oxygen, yet experiencing no brain damage beyond the disruption that had occurred to my long-term memory when I had been run over as a boy—also attested to the preternatural aspect of the event.

But why would God show me something and then not allow me to remember it? What would be the point in that, right? I can tell you that this was *the* question pressing me in the days immediately following the incident, and in my youthful naïveté and impatience, I first went about trying to find the answer to that mystery in the wrong way. I learned a valuable and biblical lesson as a result. In fact, that early mistake is why I have only just begun to tell the story of what happened that night.

A couple of days after my death and return from "over yonder," I told one of the leaders of the church that I had an important question to ask him. (This leader was not a member of the Fullers, the Osbands, or the Holtz's families.) In private, I recounted my episode and probed him for its potential meaning.

"Why would God show me something and then tell me I would not remember the vision?" I had inquired earnestly.

His response was shocking for an honest and sincere young Christian man. Basically, he suggested that I had probably eaten too much spicy food, or maybe I had accidently been poisoned and was therefore delusional or had a vivid dream.

No kidding. That was his response.

Of course, I was not yet familiar with such admonitions as, "Give not that which is holy unto the dogs, neither cast ye your pearls before swine, lest they trample them under their feet" (Matthew 7:6). Understand that I am not saying my pastor back then was a dog, but that this was a lesson I would not soon forget about sharing sacred and holy things with those who have not had similar supernatural experiences and therefore cannot appreciate or comprehend the otherworldly significance. In fact, besides my closest friends and family, from that day forward I kept the event (and what I would soon understand about its measurable implications) a secret between us.

Years later, this incident would be dragged out from secrecy and a truth behind it at least partially unveiled (at the time of this writing, I believe I will know more about this revelation in future days), but that is another story we will visit in a subsequent chapter of this memoir.

For now, suffice it to say that through this experience I had seen just a touch of heaven, just a sampling of the incomprehensible and ultra-dimensional dominion of the Lord, and the most profound stamping upon my life—which had a *purpose* for the throne of God.

My footprint was in full-steam development.

I was filling my mind with the divine truth as given to mankind through the Word of God with more tenacity and passion than I had ever searched for self-empowerment with prior. I was hungry—no, *starving*—for more Christ in my life at every turn.

I was still working for Gene Stockhoff in the harvest months, but because that didn't pay during the other seasons, I supplemented our income by working for the Archway Cookie factory nearby. During one of my shifts there, the giant Hobart mixer was whipping the dough. As I reached out to grab something, the huge machine caught me by the arm, pulled me in, and quickly severed more than half of the index and middle fingers on my left hand. The machine whirled around, yanking me about as I hollered and pulled away, and then another worker intervened and shut the power off. (My fingers were never reattached, and to this day my left hand has only two short stubs where my fingers had been.)

Shocked, I cooperated as others patched me up and sent me home to heal…but all the while, in the back of my mind, I couldn't help but think about what that machine *could have* done to me had it pulled me in farther.

At this point, everything started to fall into place: I wasn't supposed to be born; I wasn't supposed to live past that accident at four years old; I wouldn't have had the power within me to expel that evil presence from my room had I not a childhood imprint of the power of one Name; I could have easily died if that Hobart mixer had gotten near my head;

and, according to Nita's memory of that night she found me dead, I couldn't have possibly resuscitated on my own from the corpse I had become lying next to her.

God was keeping me here, keeping me functional, and keeping me safe despite all the threats of death—both physical and spiritual.

I was supposed to *do something*.

What, though, was the mystery.

Well, if I didn't yet know what my purpose was for the Lord, I was determined to start somewhere.

So, to begin with, I had seen a role at church that needed filling. Plenty of children's programs were in place, but the teens had little to do and almost no age-appropriate curriculum to delve into, should they find themselves as hungry for the Lord as I was. Immediately, I enrolled in correspondence Bible courses through the mail and poured myself into the classes at record speed. You might think that because I was going through the materials so rapidly, I couldn't really soaked up the knowledge, but that wasn't the case. In fact, it was due to my spiritual "sponge"-state that I moved as quickly as I did, drinking in every last detail of every last lesson before starting the next. I learned as much as I could during every moment when I wasn't needed as a father or husband.

While still enrolled in my classes, the pastor and I talked about the possibility of my stepping in to serve as a youth pastor. After prayerful consideration, we agreed it would benefit the church, and I became a mentor for the youth at the Amity church.

This was only the first step in tempering my steel. I didn't know what plans the Lord had for my life, but I knew on an innate level *that if I were to be used, I had to learn to be usable*. This period of my life would involve many early oratories to a young and forgiving audience.

My *first* audience.

As the years rolled by, there would be hundreds of thousands of others, as the vision God gave Nita shortly thereafter predicted. Before I tell you about that, however, there is a lesson I would like to share with you regarding this time.

After the disappointing experience of my pastor's less-than-enthusiastic response to my question regarding why God would give somebody a vision then not allow them to remember it, I struggled to make sense of what had obviously been an extraordinary incident in my and Nita's life. I prayed daily, seeking understanding, and during this same period (undoubtedly God had all this timing in control from the very beginning) I happened to be reading the Bible from cover to cover for the first time in my life. I had made it to the book of Job, and one day my eyes suddenly fell upon Job 33:15–17. The Word of God dramatically came to life in what some charismatics might call a *rhema* moment: a time when the Scripture went from being ink on paper to *the living Word of God*. The text that instantly conveyed the dynamic truth behind what had happened to me that fateful night I died read:

> In a dream, in a vision of the night, when deep sleep falleth upon men, in slumberings upon the bed; Then he openeth the ears of men, and sealeth their instruction [within them], That he may withdraw man from his purpose, and hide pride from man.

Though I was a young and inexperienced believer, I clearly understood what this text was saying to me. Like the apostle Paul who could not tell whether he was "in the body...or out of the body" when he had been "caught up to the third heaven" (2 Corinthians 12:2), God, on that momentous night, had taken me to a heavenly place and "sealed instructions" within me. These directions would be there when I needed them, as they were like a road map that the Holy Spirit would "quicken" when I could use guidance or information. Nevertheless, I was not to remember these details ahead of time; otherwise, I might be drawn away into my "own purpose" and lifted up in "pride," according to this oldest book in the Bible.

In other words, if, as a young believer, I had seen the ministries that God would later allow Nita and me to participate in, it's likely I would have made two huge mistakes: First, I would have immediately aimed at the later ministries and started working toward making them happen— all without the benefit of the struggles, trials, setbacks, side roads, and experiences that "seasoned" me and (hopefully) qualified me to eventually operate in them (thus God "withdrew me from *my* purpose"). Second, I would have been tempted by pride to think more of myself than I should have as a young man if I had envisioned winding up in high-profile ministries. So, God, in His benevolence, "hid pride" from me by keeping the revelations "sealed" until the appropriate times.

In the Bible, it is clear that God does "seal" knowledge, wisdom, and revelations in the hearts of those who follow Him. That these concealed truths can be "quickened" or made alive at the right moments as they are needed is depicted in such texts as Matthew 10:19–20, where Jesus says to His disciples: "But when they deliver you up, take no thought how or what ye shall speak: *for it shall be given you in that same hour* what ye shall speak. For it is not ye that speak, but the Spirit of your Father which speaketh *in you*" (emphasis added). That this reflects a deep partnership between our personal devotions and studies (2 Timothy 2:15; Psalm 119:11) and the indwelling Holy Spirit as part of the mystical union God holds with all members of the true Church—the Body of Christ—can also be seen in Proverbs 3:6, which says, "In all thy ways acknowledge him [that's us doing our part], and he shall direct thy paths [His part]." Again, the book of John (6:63) refers to the Holy Spirit as the one "that quickens" (Greek *zōopoieō*—"to cause to live, to make alive at that moment") the Word of God as well as those "sealed instructions" Job talked about.

If you are a sincere believer and haven't clearly received your call from God, keep seeking. It's there as surely as the Lord lives. Only within His Divine timing will your calling dawn upon you.

If, at some point, you thought that you received your calling, but it turned out to conflict with the direction your spirit felt led initially, embrace the lesson you learned during that time. No time is wasted when knowledge is being imparted. Perhaps, like me, the Lord has "locked" your ultimate call from you until He sees the moment has arrived for you to follow it. But it will only be after the preparation for the call—the benefit of the struggles, trials, setbacks, side roads, and experiences along the way—that the call will be revealed.

Finally, if you have experienced a supernatural event and later sought the advice of a ministry leader or fellow believer whose advice didn't ring true in your spirit, rest assured that the answer will come in due time. Meanwhile, pour yourself into the truth of the Word and soak up every story from those blessed pages as you can. Pray at every opportunity that you will grow in your ability to communicate with the Lord, no matter your age or circumstances. Prayer and Bible reading may not give you *an immediate* answer, but prayer and the Word *will* give you an answer, and the search will only drive you closer to the throne.

I believe this picture was taken in the office of my first pastorate in Tenmile, Oregon, around 1978.

Five

The Boy Who Put away
Childish Things

Days stretched into weeks, which stretched into months, and Nita and I were pouring our heart and soul into our youth pastor ministry. We had little money then, but we made ministry a high priority instead of applying for additional secular work. Wyoming Rosebud Dollar from Amity had almost no money of her own, but she saw two novice ministers struggling, so sprang for a brand-new copy of *Strong's Exhaustive Concordance* to help me with my Berean studies. Even back in those days, that book probably cost thirty or forty dollars, an enormous investment. However, the assistance it provided was invaluable, as it greatly enhanced my learning as well as my understanding of the original Greek and Hebrew biblical text translations. Every Wednesday night, I had a fresh observation of Scripture to share with my young audience.

About every two months or thereabouts, Nita would contact our Christian organization's district-level offices in surrounding states to see if there was an opening for a senior or associate pastor, as I was growing in my interest to preach the Gospel to as many as I could reach. Understandably, the districts continued to inform us that we were always welcome to call and inquire, but that my recommendation as senior pastor would be far more likely after I had been awarded my minister's license. So by day, I toiled in the fields and cookie factories, and by night, I dove into deep study, both personal Bible study with *Strong's* as well as my Berean classes. In the midst of this busy schedule, I discovered that just within the confines of my own family, there was quite the musical talent.

Nita had a natural knack for timing. She was simply a human metronome. Her brother, John, was groovy on the six-string guitar. I could find my way around a four-string bass alright, so between the three of us, we could produce a decent sound comparable to the popular three-chord-progression gospel sounds of that era, such as the Happy Goodmans or the Downings. All three of us could sing and harmonize, and my sister, Vidabell, was an *incredible* vocalist. Thus, our band, the "Canaan Gospel Singers," was formed.

I was still serving as the youth pastor on Wednesday nights for Amity, but on the occasional Sunday, the Canaan Gospel Singers would visit a local church during a special morning service. Our equipment was sad, to say the least. Nita literally had *one drum* (a snare), and she played it with drum-brushes, making a swishing sound instead of a traditional beat. We only had one tiny amplifier, the maximum volume of which could be outperformed by a solitary crying baby. Thankfully, many of the churches we visited had microphones, because we didn't own even one. Upon arriving at a church, I would give a brief welcome, strike up our small band for a happy little gospel number, follow it with seven or eight other original songs, and then I would wrap up with a short sermon.

People who knew us personally made calls on their own to recommend our musical ministry to other churches, and before long, we were booked almost every other Sunday to preach and play: Nita on her one drum, John on his six-string, me thumping the bass, and Vidabell serving as the central female vocalist. John and I traded the lead male vocals, and Nita harmonized whenever possible—but because of our low-quality equipment, worshippers could only hear her in very small auditoriums.

The pastorate at Amity changed when the district called Paul, our home pastor, to serve at Tenmile Assembly in Tenmile, Oregon, just fifteen miles outside of Roseburg. The Osbands took over the pastorate at Amity. Because Paul had known Nita and me, he asked us to visit Tenmile, and we did so happily. From that visit, word reached the Oregon state superintendent of our Christian organization, and he mentioned us in the district magazine. Readers of the magazine then began calling us for additional bookings.

In one of our early sets, a young couple approached us after our performance and told us that the Lord had put it on their hearts to buy us a full PA system. We were shocked, of course, especially since we never asked for anything from the churches we visited—not even an offering to help with our expenses. (The churches sometimes did gather an offering for us, but we never asked for or required it.) However, since this couple said it was the *Lord* who had told them to bless us in this way, we did not refuse, and soon afterward we had a full sound system. A friend happened to have a random, wooden tongue-and-axle trailer taking up space on his lawn. John and I took it off his hands, framing in a bed out of scrap wood to use for hauling our new equipment around. Today, I would be scared to carry anything across the yard in that contraption, but at the time, that was all we had. We carted that trailer from Oregon to Arizona to California and every place in between.

We were so blessed by all of the circumstances that were coming together for our ministry, and the more opportunities presented themselves, the more we prayed at every band practice. We didn't have a scheduled time for prayer; sometimes we would pray for thirty or forty minutes uninterrupted before we even powered up the amps. And it was during one of these prayer sessions that Nita had a vision.

Nita was, and always has been, a soft-spoken sweetheart. She would no sooner interrupt a prayer than rob a bank. Her sincere respect for the speaker was of high priority.

There we were, all four of our heads bowed, praying that God would use us to minister to the congregation the following Sunday…and Nita popped her head up, pointed right at me, and spoke right over the top of everyone.

"You're gonna preach to an unnumbered sea of people," she said.

My initial reaction was that she had chosen a very uncouth time to joke around. Not wishing to embarrass her with a rebuke, I simply chuckled it off and looked at John and Vidabell for their reaction. The air was awkward for a moment or two. They returned my smirk, but timidly so, as if they didn't know what to think of Nita's uncharacteristic disruption.

I turned back to face Nita, and her expression revealed that she was serious.

"No," I retorted. "You're kidding."

"I am *not* kidding," she said, emphatically shaking her head. "It's *going* to happen. YOU," she said reestablishing a firm finger in the air at me. "*You* are going to preach to a *sea* of unnumbered people."

I raised an eyebrow cynically, and she shook her head again as if to ardently dismiss my incoming counters of skepticism.

"Mark my words. You're going to do this."

I glanced at John and Vidabell, and they were no longer smirking. If this was a joke, it wasn't appropriate to derail prayer time for gag prophecies. But Nita wasn't the type to do that.

"I'm not kidding you. I am *not* kidding you. Don't forget this, and mark this day in your memory."

At this point, we were all at least inclined to believe that, right or wrong, Nita was convinced in her own spirit that she had seen something.

"I'm telling you this is gonna happen. It's *going to* happen," she said.

"What are you talking about?" I responded, asking the obvious question. "What is all this?"

"I saw it. It came to me just now, right now, and I saw it."

Nita went on to explain that, in her mind's eye, she had seen multitudes of people facing a single platform. "I can't even see the end of the people. They're everywhere, all over the place, as far as the eye can see. Hundreds of thousands of people," she said. At the front of the platform was a man preaching the Gospel. "It was you. *You* are the man."

Nita is not a prophetess, and she has never claimed to be, so this event was an isolated one. It's also interesting to note that she has not done anything similar since that day. Nevertheless, we all still remember the way she looked that night: So insistent. So staunch. So confident.

So *sure* of what she had seen.

"It's *going to* happen," she kept saying that night. "It's going to. Mark my words. Remember this day. I'm tellin' ya."

In the days following Nita's vision, I just decided it must be something that God was doing with her. I didn't dismiss the notion entirely that there could be some level of truth to what the Lord had revealed to her, but come on! Right? A *sea* of people? There wasn't even PA equipment in existence that could amplify my voice over a crowd that great! How could what she envisioned even be possible? And with *me* at the front? I wasn't even a licensed minister, let alone an ordained one. Me? Being trusted as a worthy mouthpiece for the Almighty God for throngs of that size?

I just didn't buy it. Not yet...

We went on with our Canaan Gospel Singers ministry, going from town to town as the blessings bestowed on us continued to increase. One day, Nita told me that she had prayed about the possibility of someday owning a drum set. She was willing to continue playing on a single snare and would live without a full set if she had to, but we all knew how much fuller our music would sound with a more varied percussion behind it, so she prayed that if it was the *Lord's* will, He would provide one for her as He had provided our PA system.

"Lord," she had prayed, "I don't know if you want me to have a full set of drums or not. I'm just feeling prompted to pray about it right now. I guess if *you* want me to have one, you will make a way. Amen."

Another one of Nita's simple prayers...and it led to another one of God's immediate answers.

I don't even remember how we ended up owning that old beater of a truck we had, but the *very next day*, the Amity pastor's son said he needed a truck, and for whatever mysterious reason, he had set his eyes on ours. The unbelievable detail of this part of the story is that he did not offer to pay us any money for the truck. Instead, he approached Nita with an offer for a trade: He would swap our timeworn pickup for a brand-spanking-new, beautiful, full set of drums.

God had provided again. Over and over, when we had nothing, He paved the way for what we needed to arrive on our doorstep at no cost to us. Undeniably, God must have approved of what we were doing, because He constantly granted us the means to continue—not just with the bare minimum, not just scraping by, but with *new* things! Pretty things! Costly things that we never had to raise money for! And this kind of provision was appearing from other angles as well. For example, there were some days when we needed a very specific amount of money; we would pray, and then God would send someone to us *with that exact amount* in hand as a "the Lord told me to do this" gesture. There were days when we needed groceries in the cabinets or gas in the tank, and even though we never announced these needs, people always came to us to put our the answer to our needs in our lap. This type of provision occurred so often that it was indisputable that the Almighty above was aware of me, aware of Nita, aware of John and Vidabell—the group who had a *purpose*—and He was showing us love in His own language.

Additionally, our ministry was really taking off. We now had drums and a sound system. More and more people were asking us to come minister to their churches, booking us out so far in the future that we had months of appearances lined up throughout the year. Each location we went to held promises of blessings both for us and the congregants, and every time our tires rolled away from a church, fresh stories were on our lips regarding those whose lives were touched through our music and my sermons. Through diligent practice, our sound had gotten tight, and we were quite a show! Our harmony was spot on. Our rhythm was synced. Our chemistry as we played off each other's energy was inspiring! We were *good*!

From seemingly everywhere all at once, people were patting us on the back, praising us for our talent, thanking us for our good works, enlightening us with their beliefs about what they just *knew* God was going to do with our lives...

At every turn, we were receiving confirmation that we were not just surviving in our evangelism, but *thriving* in it…

We were hitting the big time…

We were arriving…

We were going places…

It was as if the Lord was saying, "Thou shalt be blessed!"

Of course, as is often the way in these tales, with all this confirmation of our "amazingness" came a minor head growth. We *were* going places, but as we were busy about going and doing the Lord's business, we started to get a little big for our britches. The words "we" and "us" had begun, ever so often, to replace words like "He" and "Him." It wasn't as if we were stuffy, judgmental, better-than-you ministers, but I believe God knew that without His intervention, we may have continued to think too highly of ourselves and develop an unhealthy self-assurance. Had He not found a humorous and loving way to bring us down a notch, we, as vessels, may have continued to become full of ourselves instead of filled with *Him*. We were human, after all.

I recall the day of the humbling event as if it were yesterday…

It was as if the Lord was saying, "Thou shalt be humbled."

One Sunday, after we had greeted the congregation we were about to pour various blessings upon, I told a joke or two, broke the ice, and gave my all-too-practiced, hot-rod intro. Then John took to the microphone to dazzle the spectators with his latest original song, called "How Precious Is the Promise." It *should have* gone like this:

Years of time are swiftly passin',
bringing nearer heaven's door.
Soon, I'll be at home with Jesus,
while eternal ages roll.

After all the days of waiting,
for His voice to bid me come,
I shall walk beside my Savior,
bid bright scenes while ages roll on.

When at last our wills are spoken,
I shall meet dear ones I know,
in the presence of my Savior,
when we stand before His throne.

Oh, how precious is the promise,
that with gladness fills my soul.
I shall be at home with Jesus,
While eternal ages roll.

Instead, however, when John approached the platform and strummed the first few chords, he forgot the lyrics and fell all over himself trying to save it. What came out was *this*:

Whe-e-e-n we meet dear friends we've known,
the-e-e-n we'll meet dear friends we've known,
and whe-e-e-n we meet dear friends we've known,
the-e-e-n we'll meet dear friends we've known.

Those words stood in place of all three verses *and* the chorus. The song didn't make a lick of sense, nobody knew what was going on, and not a soul was blessed by the piece of abstract art. All John's performance had done was inspire a lot of puzzled glances and a few whispers.

When he had finished, everyone clapped (out of support, I'm sure).

I took the stage again and had a good laugh. John was embarrassed, but he was laughing, too. I made a few good-natured, elbow-in-the-ribs wisecracks—"We're all human"; "Isn't it great that we can forget the words and God loves us anyway?"; "We all make boo-boos and we're still useful in the kingdom"—and each of my statements received a hearty "amen," applause for God's graciousness, and some light-hearted chuckling. From the stage, all faces were smiling with understanding and encouragement.

And you never can tell. Maybe *John* needed a humbling that day.

Then it was my turn…and it was so much worse.

I adjusted the microphone stand to my height, tightened it (or so I thought…), grabbed the guitar, and began to play another "special." It ended up being very, *very* special. A performance to remember, no doubt about it.

The song was called "Caught Up Together," and thankfully I remembered every word of it, because, as it turned out, I hardly needed any further contributions to my own demise. Through the first verse, everything went smoothly. However, at the chorus turnaround, the height adjustment of the mic stand came a little loose, and ever so slowly, the mic began to descend, lower and lower, one centimeter at a time. My hands were on the guitar, so I couldn't pull it back up.

At first, it was no big deal; I just hunkered down a little and kept playing.

"We're gonna be caught up together on that Resurrection day…"

At the beginning of the second verse, the mic slipped down farther, running away from my mouth with the speed of a snail…lowering, sinking…and I found myself playing and singing in a hunchback position, towering over the stand. By the second chorus round, I had bent my knees, standing at a half squat. The audience was trying to be polite, but here and there, you could see people hiding their giggles behind purses and tithing envelopes.

"We're gonna be caught up together on that Resurrection day…"

The third verse found me using muscles in my legs I didn't even know I had. My body wasn't built for prolonged half-squat poses. Nobody came to the platform to fix my mic, so I just kept on "performing." Eventually, I gave in to my legs' shaky mercy petitions and collapsed to my knees. *Now*, however, the mic was several inches too high, I had to stretch my neck like an ostrich to reach it, and my words were cut short and delivered with little confidence. There I was, Mr. Big-Time Minister, looking like a small child asking for a cookie. The snickering across the building was now developing into a full laugh, and people everywhere were slapping their hands to their thighs…and it *wasn't* because of my excellent, toe-tapping rhythm.

"We're gon… gonna be caught up to—together on that Resur… rection day…"

We were caught up alright… What a spectacle!

When my comedy act ended, I stood, adjusted that infuriating microphone stand, cranked it until my knuckles were white, and then faced the audience with a sheepish grin. *Everyone* was falling apart in their seats. I joined them in their amusement like a good sport, cracking a few more jokes about God having a sense of humor. Internally, I was mortified, but I played it off and moved right along. Oh, thank *goodness* it was Vidabell's turn. She was fantastic at remembering lyrics, she had both hands free in case of a mic-stand malfunction, her voice sounded like an angel, and the song she was about to sing was grand. With all of us at our instruments behind her, and with her graceful talents, there was no way we could fail. I was just *sure* that she was going to redeem our morning.

In my lifetime I have felt "sure" of a lot of things.

Sometimes it just doesn't pan out.

John started us off with a placid strum, a rapturous chiming that flowed across the hall like an acoustic waterfall. Nita fused in with delicate cymbals and the tender swishing of her brushes, the tinkling of bells amongst a gentle breeze. My first bass note brought in the backbone, carrying the other sounds as a strong and steady ship upon the ripples of the ocean. It was soft, tantalizing, and serene.

In the crowd, husbands placed their arms around their wives. Ladies smiled and nodded peacefully with the calm tempo. The pastor leaned back quietly in the pew and placed one leg over the other in anticipation of a touching refrain. As the notes rang from our hands and into the atmosphere, one could almost hear the unspoken "hallelujah" that rested on the air like a silent praise just waiting to be released at the peak of the melody.

Vidabell started to sway… her eyes closed. Her elegant skirt rocked back and forth. Her long, pretty fingers with freshly polished nails touched the silver shine on the microphone ever so slightly and lifted it from its cradle as she leaned in. Her chest swelled with an intake of breath. Her lips parted, and for three words it was the prettiest thing you'd ever heard…

But then, in an appropriate culmination of what was starting to look like a stand-up routine, her voice gave out. Shehe choked. By word five, she was crackling and gulping and wheezing and sputtering. She tried to recover, but it was a lost cause. The words she *did* sing sounded more like a frog with a head cold than a vocalist. (Poor Vidabell…she really was an amazing singer.)

Certainly, it wasn't her fault, and there was nothing she could have done to prevent it. All performers choke at some point, right? We could simply play eight measures and round back up to a second beginning while she cleared her throat. It would be an easy fix.

But what she chose to do next turned out to be the icing on the cake. Without a word, without a laugh, without even so much as a smile, she shoved the microphone on its stand and ran to the front pew, covering her face with her hands. Nita, John, and I shared awkward glances and for a moment we continued, giving her the opportunity to come back and try again. It looked for a split second like she was going to gather her wits and return when she took a deep breath and lowered her hands to her lap. But then, she just sat there, unmoving, and stared at us, while *we* were playing *her* song! (Later, when I asked Vidabell why in the world she had run off the stage at the beginning of her song without giving it another shot, her answer was, "I don't know! I don't know why I did that! I just freaked out!" Today, when asked, she said, "Yes, I remember that big debacle. I guess I just figured we were stinkin' the place up and it was time to just let Joe preach and get outta there.")

I shook my head and stopped playing, and John and Nita followed suit. There was no recovering. No pat jokes about God's humor or our boo-boos were going to save us now. We could see expressions of pity and concern from the audience, and rather than to try another go-round and potentially give Nita a turn to humiliate herself, I just decided our little concert was over. Nita and John took their seats next to Vidabell, and I started preaching. I don't even remember now what I said, because the rest of the service was a blur. As soon as the clock hands pointed to twelve, I bowed in prayer and got off of that stage as diplomatically as possible. It all happened in around thirty minutes from my hot-rod introduction to the tail-tuck retreat. The only redeeming quality of that morning was that my recently shrunken britches had an easier time carrying my now-deflated head.

And that's what God does sometimes, isn't it? When things get out of proportion, He reins it back in and puts it in its place. As Nita says, "We'll never forget that day when everything went stupid."

Overall, the church members were very forgiving. Prior to our final retreat, when the service had been dismissed by the pastor, we were inundated with kind words and sincere handshakes. It was more than obvious that we had experienced an off day. To the congregants' credit, they realized that—and to our gain, they were understanding and supportive. We were so grateful that, even when we had spoiled everything, we still left feeling accepted. They knew we had meant well, that we had not intentionally turned their morning service into the clown show it became, and that our ministry was valuable beyond what proof we had offered them. The benefit of the doubt they gave us was the only good that came out of that whole ordeal, aside from the slice of humble pie we evidently needed to chew on for a while.

In any case, our ministry didn't stop there. We followed through with our bookings, and in due course we recouped our self-esteem as a group. Eventually, though, after a *great* run of it, John and Vidabell went in their own directions. Nita and I opted for an alternative music ministry using prerecorded accompaniment tapes. Because of the injury to my hand at Archway Cookies, it was a significant challenge for me to play an instrument anyway, so the tapes were a valuable crutch. Allie had become old enough to sing as well, so she presented a few songs specifically written for a lighthearted child.

Pretty soon, however, our days of traveling ministry became more difficult as Nita's belly was growing heavy with another member of the family. We didn't take much time off when she had the baby, but when my son Joe was born, he was such a delight that we jumped at the opportunity to show him off. We were back on the road for a while, and Allie was being homeschooled.

In the meantime, I completed my Berean studies and received my minister's license. Nita had kept up with the district phone calls, and one day she was given a new update: Tenmile needed a pastor. Paul, Amity's previous pastor, had gone to Tenmile, and upon his decision to leave (the reason is unclear), he recommended us as his replacement. The district leaders knew that the Canaan Gospel Singers had visited Tenmile in the past, and they were aware that we had been recommended as traveling evangelists all over the West Coast, so when our names were suggested, they quickly approved. Paul called and gave us the rundown.

"That church has been struggling for *years*," he said. "I don't want you to feel any pressure to make snap decisions, but I also want you to be informed of the district's assessment of the situation. If you and Nita choose not to take the pastorate at Tenmile, they're closing it down."

Nita and I visited the church and were surprised to see that by our second attendance there, it had a total congregation of eight people when all members were present. When our names were put to a vote, all eight approved. We gave them a one-year commitment.

Our experience in moving to and settling in at Tenmile presented us with many true miracles. The first miracle involved our mobile home. In order to relocate, we needed to obtain enough money for me to be able to quit my job and start over. Tenmile was a three-hour drive away. Within only days of listing the home we had placed on Gene Stockhoff's land, a man offered to pay us what it had cost us brand new years prior, and he even paid to have it moved to another lot. Nita and I both had the same gut feeling (which we later confirmed was a Holy-Spirit motivation) we should deposit the money we made from that sale (around ten grand) in a savings account for sometime in our future, but that, for now, we should live on faith.

The second miracle was a *literal* play-out of the popular "seed money/ law of tenfold return." I don't believe in the "prosperity gospel" and "prosperity preaching," and I don't believe that a person should *ever* give on the promise that his or her money will be returned ten times over. However, during this era of my life, such an occurrence happened for me and Nita around the same time, and with separate—but similar—circumstances. A man from our tiny Tenmile church approached me with what was known back then as "the Gospel handshake." Clasped in his palm when he gripped my own was a twenty-dollar bill. He told me that he just felt the Lord had told him to give it to Nita and me. I thanked him sincerely for what was at that time such a huge gift. That bill was still in my wallet later in the week when I attended a district meeting. An offering for a missionary was being collected there, and I heard a still, small voice inside prompting me to give it all to the collection. After doing so, I kid you not, within *one week*, I received ten checks from pastors all across Oregon, each in the amount of exactly twenty dollars, and each including notes that said the likes of, "I just felt the Lord was putting it on my heart to send this to you and Nita." When Nita and I received our tax return of about seventy-five dollars, I gave her a five-dollar bill and told her to spend all of it on herself. She walked down to the store, bought a snack, and had four dollars left. Then, Sunday morning rolled around, and she heard a still, small voice inside prompting her to give all four dollars to the children's Sunday school offering. After doing so, between Sunday school and the main service, she ran to the parsonage to grab something she needed. A woman from church followed her there, saying, "Sister Horn, I just felt the Lord told me to do something this morning." She gave Nita the Gospel handshake, slipping her exactly forty dollars.

Things like this kept happening. An elderly woman who lived off of her food stamps couldn't give anything monetarily, but when she went to the store, she would spend ten percent of her food stamps on our family and the church as her tithe. To this day, Allie remembers that she had prayed in her sweet little heart for very specific groceries—Honeycombs and Lucky Charms cereal with milk were part of one prayer request she remembers well—and on more than one occasion, this woman would appear on our doorstep with exactly the items we needed to get through the week... including Allie's cereal.

These instances may not have involved great healings, powerful signs, and ultimate wonders (although at times those events happened as well, but that's another story for another time), but we saw God's hand in everything we were doing there. He met every need we had over and over again through direct intervention and often through the use of His people. We never went hungry, we never froze, and we were always moderately comfortable that year—despite the fact that, when the year was over and we looked at our next tax return, we couldn't fathom how we had ever survived it. In the beginning, the church was not paying us a dime. During our pastorate there, however, the church grew by leaps and bounds, reaching well beyond its seating capacity of seventy-seven people. By the time we left that church, an average attendance of one hundred and twenty people was the norm—up from *eight*! All the children had to sit on the floor in the front of the sanctuary by the pulpit, and the young men would lean against the walls and in a crisscross position down the aisles. Eventually we did start drawing a salary of $250 per month, but our tax records still didn't make sense.

There is no feasible way that a family of four could live off of our income. One miraculous provision after another kept us afloat in His service—and this time, we had "the day of the great humbling event" fresh on our minds, so we gave credit where credit was due and never allowed ourselves to inflate over our own works.

When our commitment at Tenmile was fulfilled, we prayed about whether we should stay or go. Church membership was exploding beyond what the walls were capable of accommodating. I felt like I was being led away from pastoring that church toward something else I was supposed to do, but I didn't want to leave them in a lurch, so I sought to place together some fundraising channels before I even talked about any goodbyes.

Around that time, I ended up with a very important phone number in my possession. Today, I can't remember how I obtained it, but I think I recall someone giving me this phone number and encouraging me to call and ask about whether the person would be willing to donate to a building fund. When I called, the man on the other end of the line gave me a cordial greeting. Before I told him of our church situation, I learned that this man went by the endearing name "Pappy."

"Old Pappy Ford, they call me."

"My name's Tom. It's nice to meet you. Thank you so much for taking my call today."

I had *no idea* this man from Roseburg was a multibillionaire who owned almost all the Weyerhaeuser property along the coastlines from Portland, Oregon, to the California border. In fact, had I any clue of that, I would have been terrified to call him in the first place. When I explained my church situation, he gave me a considerate response.

"I'll tell you what I'll do," he said. "You get your blueprints ready, and when you're all set to build, you come in and see me and we'll talk about it." That was all he said, but I could tell from his kind voice that he was legitimately interested in helping me; his response was not at all a casual dismissal.

I never spoke to Pappy again, but it was not the last time that he would be central in my ministry. Shortly after that phone call, I learned how wealthy he was. It blew my mind that I had so informally dialed him up and asked about his interest in donating to a church fund. When I met with the district leadership about our choice to move on, I gave them all the information regarding Pappy Ford and the blueprints, and they agreed to follow up on it.

As Nita and I were preparing to leave Tenmile, not yet exactly knowing what we were going to do next, we happened by a couple on the side of the road. They were driving a really nice, brand-new, twenty-two-foot travel trailer when a big semi-truck had forced them to swerve, sending the front end of their vehicle into a post. I pulled over to make sure they were okay and see if they needed someone to go for help. (We didn't have cell phones in those days.) Both the man and his wife were perfectly fine, although they were understandably disgruntled about the fact that their trailer was badly damaged. We talked for a while about the accident, and Nita and I waited there with them until help arrived. Before we left, I gave him the man home phone number in case he and his wife needed anything in the coming days. Oddly, he gave me his number in return, which I didn't quite understand, but I didn't refuse.

Placing his number in my wallet, I wished them both good luck, got back in the car, and drove away. The next day I saw their trailer in the same spot on the road, covered in caution tape. I decided to check in on the man to see if all was well, and he responded, "Yeah, the thing's totaled. The insurance is just gonna pay us for it." Later in the same conversation, he offered this strange follow-up: "Hey, you know… If you had any use for that trailer, you could probably call the insurance company and see if they would be willing to sell it for real cheap. They're prolly just gonna have it squashed at the yard anyway."

What an idea…

Nita and I had been talking about the possibility of returning to our roles as traveling evangelists, so I asked a metal worker from our church to go look at the wrecked vehicle with me to see if the damage was even remotely repairable. One glance at it and this man from church was convinced.

"Oh man, Tom. This is an *easy* fix! All we would need is some new steel for the tongue here on the front, a little reframing, pop the dent right outta there, and you'd have yourself a perfectly functional trailer."

We went inside and saw that everything was in mint condition. The cabinets near the front had fallen onto a bed below, but they, too, were in great shape—during the impact, they had simply popped off the walls; a few screws would make them fully functional again.

When I called the insurance company, I didn't let myself get my hopes up. The rig might have been damaged, but in good condition it would have easily been worth twenty grand. The likelihood that the company would offer a price within our range was a long shot. But the victory jig I danced when I got off the phone let Nita know that the offer was within our means: three hundred dollars. *Three hundred!* Not three thousand, three *hundred*… That was the asking price, because the insurance company didn't want to mess with repairing it for sale. I forced myself to contain my excitement until the dial tone from the receiver told me I was safe to celebrate.

"Woohoo! Oh-ho-ho, what a steal!"

For three bills, Nita and I had a portable home, a *nice* one with a shower, a stove, and a working bathroom. We couldn't believe it. Another precious church saint allowed us to park the trailer on her lawn while the metal worker restored it for us for next to no cost.

With our future decided and the Tenmile church in good hands, we said loving goodbyes and took to the road again, this time for almost three years. During the weeks, we traveled and put our hands to use any good way we could, including leading occasional Wednesday night services, and on the weekends we would minister at churches where we had been invited to preach. As before, Nita, Allie, and I (Joe was still too little) sang to accompaniment tapes—and afterward, I would give a sermon. As in our earlier tours, we were welcomed with open arms and recommendations followed. And as before, we never missed a meal, and God provided all of our needs.

We truly were blessed.

After I had waited through the mandatory observational period to become a licensed minister, I attended the district council and left as an ordained minister. When we stopped shortly after that for a camp meeting in Salem, Oregon, we discovered that another church was in in need of a pastor—Cornerstone Church in Crescent City, California. I absolutely *did not* want to go there. I don't know if secretly I lacked confidence, or if it was because it was so far away from the people and territory I knew, but for some reason I did not like the possibility of taking a church in Northern California. We had a lot on our minds, we had a lot going on, and we were moving in a completely different direction.

I prayed like a child.

"Lord, please don't let this door open. You know I don't want to go to Crescent City. It's not my calling, Lord. Right? It's not my calling. Please don't let this happen. Just help them find another pastor. I'm claiming this now, that they are just going to *find* who they need and it's not going to involve me."

Be careful the things you "claim"…

One day not long after my prayer, we received a phone call.

It was a gentleman from Cornerstone Church who had heard about

Nita and me, knew about our ministries, and had become aware that we were calling the local districts in search of a new pastorate. As if on cue, he asked if we would consider filling the open position at Cornerstone.

Boy, I had a feeling about that one…

Unwilling to belligerently disobey the Lord's calling on my life, I agreed to at least visit the church, "put the feelers out," and see what would happen. And from behind the wheel, all the way to Crescent City, I prayed…

"Lord, please close this door. You know I don't want to do it, Lord. Close this door. I am just praying, right here, right now, that you will close this door and open something else for me. You know my heart, and you know this is not the desires of it."

When I arrived at the church, I saw the sanctuary had seating for about 250 people, and it was crowded. Nita and I timidly and dutifully took our family to the front pew, where we had been invited to sit. Reluctantly, I waited for the service to start. I presented myself pleasantly, but on the inside, I continued to offer my childish prayer.

Because the church's previous pastor had already moved on, a board member went to the platform, greeted the congregation warmly, made a few brief announcements, and then revealed that it was time for worship. I watched as a woman approached the piano, settled herself on the bench, and began to play an upbeat tempo piece.

Wow… She's pretty good, I thought. I hadn't come with any expectations at all, but when this pianist's fingers got to moving, some amazing sounds filled the air. Elsewhere on the stage, a man started to pluck around on a bass guitar, and his trilling on the low notes put my best bass licks to shame. Another instrumentalist stepped forward with a southern-style harmonica strain that canvassed the perfect introduction for the dynamic organist on the other end of the platform to subsequently burst in with a powerhouse minor chord that harmonized every other sound together like the final glue over a complicated jigsaw puzzle.

A door opened beside the platform, and around forty people entered, clapping on rhythm. A few belted out random, inspiring arias as they filtered in and took their designated places on stage. Once there, they stepped back and forth to the beat. With a rising crescendo from the piano landing on a huge, climactic bang, the choir members opened their mouths and just *howled* forth praise! Deep, moving, perfect-pitch voices blew like a trumpet blast so incredible I was surprised this church still had all its windows intact. The power of the music wasn't just in its volume—although the singers weren't lacking in that area. The impact came from the passion and feeling that poured from their hearts and flew through the air as powerfully as the winds of a violent tornado… but instead of raining down destruction, *this* tornado rained down a Holy-Spirit craving.

I had seen choirs like this in the movies, but they had usually been in African-American Southern Gospel churches. This church was filled with mostly white folks, and I wouldn't have guessed they were capable of expressing such soul! I mean, there's just no describing it. They dumbfounded me, knocked that childish chip right off my shoulder, and stomped it into oblivion. Within seconds of listening to their hearts explode from their chests in one of the most anointed worship songs I've ever heard, my thoughts of resisting being called to serve at this church were wiped straight out of my head. My trepidations became nonexistent in light of this hymn.

I looked at Nita, and her eyes were like baseballs. Seven-year-old Allie was clapping and cheering, and three-year-old Joe was dancing as if this was the first time he had experienced music.

I looked around, and all of the worshippers were standing to their feet, joining the choir in a vibrant, energetic atmosphere that pulsed the floor underneath me. These congregants weren't just praising the Lord, they were animatedly thrusting their arms to the ceiling and stomping and hollering and shouting and *living* praise!

I'm telling you. It cannot be described. The words in this book cannot do it justice.

I lifted my hands into the air and surrendered. The music covered my audible prayers, shrouding them in silence from those around me, but I prayed them just the same.

"Lord, *please* open this door! This is my calling, Lord! This is where I'm supposed to be! You know the desires of my heart, and this is it! Oh God, I just pray you will open this door for my family! Please God, open this door!"

As history tells, that door opened, my name was cast to a vote, and the results were unanimous. I pastored that church for some of the greatest years of my life, making many memories—including serving as the head of the minister's association in that area as well as welcoming the birth of my youngest daughter, Donna.

I laugh at myself now when I think of my words to God in those days. When the Word speaks of the Lord "knowing the desires of our hearts" (Psalm 37:4), it also means that many times He knows them better than we do, and He knows the lessons we have to learn on the way to achieving them, lest our precious treasures be cast on swine because we don't know how to appreciate the desires that arrive too early. We best not tear a butterfly from a cocoon before it has fully transformed. Such was unquestionably the case for my tenure at Cornerstone, because that time in my life wasn't *just* about pastoring Cornerstone, but about the other tools I was given there for later on. How grateful I am today that I was at least obedient enough to consider it as a possibility, as it was from that era that I was introduced to just fledgling concepts of the work I do today.

For several years prior to my time at Cornerstone, I had been listening to Southwest Radio Church radio broadcasts with Noah Hutchings. I learned *so much* about theology from his show, and he was way ahead of his time in his willingness to tackle issues such as science, space, extraterrestrials, etc., from a biblical worldview. Many people who would never darken the doorway of a church—people who had questions that the Church simply wouldn't address in a traditional setting—"attended" the Hutchings "church services" from their own comfortable living rooms and vehicles…. Turns out this *was* a church. It may not have been built with a foundation of concrete or stone, but it was a church just the same, with unity and camaraderie, discipleship, and shepherding of the flock. Likewise, this type of church service didn't have the same impact on the pastoral family as a brick-and-mortar church would, since it did not include the conflicts and administrative duties that go along with ministry from a building. In a broadcast format, the speaker could preach from his heart, never clouded with the worries of offending certain influential members of his church body, as those who didn't agree had the right to change the station. Further, the message given over the airways could reach an enormous—literally unlimited—congregation. Little by little, this "radio church" idea was imprinting within my psyche the efficacy of nontraditional pastoring.

The only significantly obvious obstacle I was able to see about this unique ministry avenue was that it didn't pay a plugged nickel until a pastor had been in the media long enough to build a financial infrastructure that would support his or her family. I had certainly taken a leap of faith before, and God had taken care of me and my own, but as for launching a new enterprise through Christian media in the early 1980s, I didn't feel the timing was right to abandon everything for the unknown. I had not yet emerged from my cocoon where that was concerned, and the Lord had some lessons to teach me before I could be useful in that area full time. That didn't stop me, however, from sticking a toe in the water when the opportunity presented itself.

Rob Thompson, my associate pastor, had heard about a small television station that broadcasted from the center of the city. I don't remember exactly how we pulled the strings to get a spot there, but shortly after Rob and I inquired at the station, we were putting on a thirty-minute show. I can't tell you how many homes the broadcast reached, but this was my first reccurring appearance on television. In addition, KCRE, a country radio station in the area, gave me a thirty-minute broadcast spot in prime time daily. Its radio tower was, at that time, a very powerful one, with one hundred thousand watts. (A "powerful" radio tower in those days might have been only twenty-five thousand watts.) Located as close to the coastline as it was, it would hit what they called "radio skip," wherein the signal would skip across the ocean to Canada, Latin America, Mexico, and several other surrounding land masses. As a result, my show was heard all over the place. We received letters from foreign listeners on a fairly regular basis. The publicity for this program eventually caught the attention of someone over at *The 700 Club* show, because it was during this era when they had me on to share my conversion testimony.

From the work the Lord was doing through me, people were hearing the Gospel message, and Cornerstone grew rapidly. Soon we had no choice but to start knocking down walls, building bigger bathrooms, and extending the exterior of the church to accommodate the crowd. For a good chunk of my time there, some section of the building was always under construction. Eventually we wrote out plans to buy the lot across the road and completely rebuild, an idea that gained support from many sides. Nita and I, however, began to feel that even though we thoroughly loved our position at Cornerstone and cherished its people, something was calling us away from Crescent City.

We had felt this for some time. On the one hand, there appeared to be no reason to ever leave, as we couldn't have designed a more comfortable life had we sat down and written our dreams on paper, word for word. On the other hand, we never felt anything specific, a needling discomfort set in that had us questioning whether our ministry might ultimately be elsewhere—and, as God had already shown us by bringing our family to Crescent City in the first place, *He* knew what we wanted even more than we did.

Once again, after making sure that blueprints and funding and building plans were in the hands of those who were more than happy to oversee the expansions and more than qualified to do so, Nita and I packed our bags to leave, having no idea where we were going or what we would do next. Our departure from Cornerstone was the most heartbreaking of all others before or since. Nita shed so many tears when we left, and for years afterward, every time the pastor's chair became vacant, the church would call us and ask us to return, and Nita would just cry.

Nonetheless, there is no doubt in our minds that it was time for us to move on, because it would only be a couple more very educational pit stops on the journey before we arrived in Missouri to launch the ministries we have in force today.

For a short time, we drove around a bit, called surrounding districts, and prayed. Several churches were looking for a pastor, and we visited them with an open mind, but something didn't feel right about each one in turn. Then a church called Life Center contacted me to send a résumé, which I did. They subsequently invited me to preach a sermon, kind of like an audition, and I agreed. This time around, it felt like the right fit for all involved, and when I submitted my name for vote, I was given the pastorate. I did not know at the time that my role would not simply be as a preacher.

Because the previous pastor of Life Center was preaching his last sermon the weekend Nita and I arrived in the area ready to get to work, we decided to let him have one final Sunday alone with his congregation. With a new church position beginning in one week and having nowhere else to go, Nita and I loaded up the kids and drove up and down the nearby roads looking for a church to visit just for fun. Rounding a corner just a mile or so away from Life Center, we saw an enormous church with a big sign that said "Evangel Chapel" and decided it would suffice for a one-time deal.

Parking the car, I was instantly overwhelmed with the feeling that I needed to stay in the car and pray. About *what*, I didn't know, but I told Nita to take the kids inside and she graciously followed my instinct. Once alone, I prayed throughout the duration of the service that the Lord would reveal to me what I was supposed to take away from this sensation. My eyes were squinting, but not completely closed, when I saw a shadow fall across the bottom of my windshield. I looked up and saw that a man had approached, but he wasn't completely corporeal, nor did he appear to be an angel or spirit of any kind. He was more like a partially transparent, but otherwise totally regular, man. Even with my windows rolled up, I could hear him when he spoke: "We need to merge with you."

When I blinked, he was gone.

I had never seen this person before, I had never even seen this church before, and I had only rolled into this area the day before, so I couldn't have already met anyone who would have subconsciously entered my imagination. But, he had unique, sharp, bird-like features and wavy, brown, 1970s-disco-styled hair that I would not forget.

Nita and the kids returned to the vehicle a few minutes later.

"I have to tell you something," I said when she opened the door. "I don't know what just happened, but I guarantee you this church and the church that we're going to pastor are going to merge."

She was naturally confused, but when I told her what I had seen, she believed it to be true also. However, we kept that incident a secret, so as not to set events in motion before their due time.

A month into my work at Life Center, a member of the board at Evangel Temple called me and said he and others at their church wanted to talk to me about a merger. I was speechless, but still didn't say a word about the partly see-through man who had approached my car. The board member explained that they were having trouble with their current pastor: He had been caught having an extramarital affair, and because this was causing all kinds of drama and dissention within the church, they were planning to discharge him. Their idea, which was supported by our organization's district, was to merge right away and allow *me* to be the pastor of both churches. I knew I had been given a clear word from the Lord that a merger would eventually happen, but the timing of what they were suggesting felt wrong because they hadn't yet dismissed their current pastor. Further, I had only just arrived at Life Center and didn't want to bombard my new congregation with talk of moving things around so dramatically just yet. As a compromise with the Evangel Temple committee, I said, "When your church finds another pastor, I promise I will contact him and we can talk about a merge."

In the meantime, Evangel Temple continued to try to work out the problems with its current leadership, and the situation worsened until the church's leadership finally found another man to fill the pastorate.

The man they elected, Bob, was like me: He wanted to wait to settle in before moving things around.

So more time passed.

After a year or two, just as with Tenmile and Cornerstone, our Life Center church was busting at the seams. While I was facing yet another potential construction project, the word came again from that gigantic Evangel Temple that times were falling hard on them financially, their congregation was dwindling, and they were looking to merge with us. Bob and I talked with the district and learned more about their situation.

Several years earlier, some bad decisions had been made when the former Evangel Temple leadership went against the district's suggestions and built a church larger than needed in an area down the road from many other places of worship. Their motive had been to basically absorb all of the community into one megachurch, but it didn't go down like they had planned, and now they were left with astronomical debt. Between that struggle and all the division that had occurred as a result of the previous pastor's indiscretions, the church had diminished to only about thirty-five or forty regular attenders.

Life Center, on the other hand, was growing like crazy, and we needed a *much* larger building. With the money we had pouring into saving accounts by those who gave to the church, taking on the debt of a mortgage for a brand-new, already-built church made more sense than beginning construction of a new one.

Now the timing felt right.

After we presented the idea to our congregations and they agreed to the merge, Bob and I brought all the attendees together in Evangel Temple to make the vote official. The second I walked in to shake hands with the board, I met Jim—a man with unique, sharp, bird-like features and wavy, brown, 1970s-disco-styled hair. I greeted him politely, and when I was out of earshot, I turned to Nita.

"That's him. That's the guy who came to my car that day and then disappeared."

My only guess about why God had given me a vision of him specifically was that there was no confusing him with anyone else. But, other than his previous, apparition-like appearance at the car, the day of the merger vote was the first time I had ever seen him.

The vote was cast and approved, and Bob and I were invited to the pulpit to share follow-up words for our newly formed congregation. Now that the decision was final, I shared with everyone what had happened on that first Sunday in the city. When I finished the story, everyone was amazed and took it as confirmation that this merger was meant to be. Later, Jim verified to many that he had never approached my car in the parking lot, had never spoken a word of merger to me, and in fact had never even met me before the vote.

So, as it turned out, I hadn't been called to that area *just* to pastor a church, but to oversee the bringing together of two churches in a mutually beneficial arrangement that potentially saved one and greatly blessed the other. Together, we worshiped in Evangel Temple, which was renamed Family Worship Center.

After the merger, Bob and I worked together very well. He enjoyed the administrative side of associate pastoring, but didn't like to preach as much. I, on the other hand, was willing to preach in those days, but dreaded the administrative work. We made a great team, church attendance grew quickly, and soon we packed out the auditorium with celebrity-status ministers from Turner Broadcasting Television Network (TBN) who visited to speak regularly.

Had I listened to the voices of those around me, I would still be pastoring to this day, and likely still at Family Worship Center. Had I used fruitful ministries as a measuring stick, the result would also be the same. Yet, after another few years there, again despite our love for the incredible people and great comfort in our position, Nita and I got that old familiar feeling—that "we're needed elsewhere" feeling that always led to the packing of bags and uprooting of lives.

By now, though, we were not afraid of this feeling. We embraced it knowing that it could only lead to walking in the will of God, and that would benefit all involved. Additionally, although I had enjoyed watching my kids grow up in ministry, the life of a pastor's child can be trying, and I could see they were becoming exhausted by it as well. Nita had been a pastor's wife for nearly our entire marriage—and we had no intention of leaving the ministry—but a change of pace would be welcome.

I knew that whatever ministry God placed on my lap next would involve my family, as even my kids had assisted in all the programs at Family Worship Center. But the *extent* of their involvement was not something I could have planned. I had no idea when I drove away from Family Worship Center for the last time that the next bend in our lives would be the birth of a familial cohesion raising the bar above everything our wildest dreams could have visualized…

Sometimes God leads us down a path we can't possibly comprehend, and then pulls us out of it and redirects, just when everything appears to be exactly what we think it should be.

Sometimes, we pray like children: "Please Lord, don't let that door open!" And all the while, God is smiling, knowing that later on we will be dancing a jig when we realize what He had planned all along.

Sometimes, He gives the people around us gut feelings, words of wisdom, or even visions that we will accomplish something we can't wrap our minds around, like taking the Gospel to a "sea of unnumbered people."

But in order to witness the wonders that await, we eventually need to stop speaking and understanding and thinking like a child, stop putting limitations on God, and "put away childish things" (1 Corinthians 13:11). Then, and only then—when we can truly pray "Your will be done, Lord" and mean it with the fullness of our hearts, souls, and minds—will we achieve our utmost. It goes farther than just trusting that the Lord will provide for our needs like He did for the McLaughlins, Mom, Nita, and me. It means trusting Him that even in *ministry* we may be yanked in different directions, made to encounter all sorts of issues, placed in leadership positions that promise to be long-term, and then plucked away like Philip from the pool with the Ethiopian eunuch and transported to another city when the Holy Spirit chooses.

What then became of the "sea of unnumbered people"?

What you are about to read in the next pages is the last and final curve. We—Nita, Allie, Joe, Donna, and myself—*all* had lessons to learn from the next pit stop on the way to where we are now. Today, I look back on the lives of each of us and it blows my mind that I was blind to it all these years. As all of the members of my family have grown and developed in the Lord, they have shown predispositions in their characters that I thought were treasurable, but when blended together it was a motley mix. If anything, each would have his or her *own* ministry, and I would be happy to help in those endeavors any way I could. But all together? It didn't make sense that we would all be using such diverse talents and callings from opposite ends of the spectrum while traveling on the *same* ministerial road. I wasn't creative enough to see how it would all work together.

That is, until we *saw* them working together, naturally, beautifully, as if each of us had been chosen to glide in the same direction for a complementary purpose but with a tremendously varied approach.

Footprints—each one distinct from the other, but walking toward an identical goal...

The goal of the Great Commission for an unnumbered sea of people.

Six

The Boy Whose Purpose
Became Known

After leaving Family Worship Center, having decided to retire from traditional pastoral roles, Nita and I invested in real estate for a season. It was an area in which we had developed interest and skills through the years. Not only had we remodeled several churches, but while our children were young, buying, remodeling, and reselling foreclosure homes had been a way to supplement our incomes when my church salary wasn't quite enough.

We had lived around the Gresham, Oregon, area for a time, flipping homes and leasing commercial sites for small businesses. Most often we lived in the houses while we worked on them, so my children all have distinct memories of their belongings always existing under a fine layer of sheetrock dust or random glops of drywall mud. We moved so often that we took house-hunting trips as frequently as other families might go yard-sale hopping. Once in a while, Nita and I would stumble across a small business that needed an administrative remodel, so we would buy it, completely redesign its trade structures, operate the company long enough to establish a record of steadily increasing revenue, and then sell it for a higher price than what we paid.

However, my heart was never in the secular work like it had been in ministry. At the end of each long day, I would toss my carpet tacks and framing nails aside and slip into the practice of theological refining. Every time I found something thought-provoking, I would make a note of it and then spend each free moment I had developing a deep analysis, eventually accumulating these insights and transcribing them into little blurbs of my own writing. The longer I studied, the more I realized that the topics that fascinated me also happened to be the same subjects the Church wasn't typically addressing. I started to notice a concerning trend. A *lot* of folks were searching for answers to questions the Church just wasn't focusing on.

For example, a friend of mine expressed his recent claim of occultism and linked it to a supernatural event that his former Christian pastor said was a result of overactive imagination. I discreetly ran to the Bible and looked up every verse on the subject and prayed…prayed…prayed.

I also heard of a woman who otherwise would have led a God-fearing life, but because her family member had come forward with a story of alien abduction, she no longer believed that God's Word holds all the answers. Once again, I ran to my study corner to read…read…read.

All around me, it was evident that although the Church was preaching the Gospel and helping others in their times of need, there were a few niche groups the Church wasn't even equipped to reach.

I knew I didn't have all the answers, but if I could even make an impact on *one person* as a result of Bible study in what the Church would consider "fringe" topics, then all the efforts in the world were worth it.

Noah Hutchings' voice continued to fill the atmosphere of every working environment I created. While I was patching holes in walls and running revenue reports, my radio speakers were blaring the latest episode of *Southwest Radio Church*. Noah's words were always heard over the commotion of my workplace, and they were increasingly powerful: "God is on the throne, and prayer changes things." I listened while he boldly tackled "fringe" subjects without apology. As we were moving all over the state and working many a Sunday, regular church attendance became more difficult than it had been in the past, so I became a congregant of the Southwest Radio Church crowd. So influenced was I by Noah's boldness that I began to feel my wings spreading into those subjects that the average Church leaders wouldn't touch.

In the mid 90s, I wrote my first book, *Spiritual Warfare: The Invisible Invasion*. In it, I focused on the occultism driven by the New Age approach to spirituality that appeared to be dominating the nation at that time. By 1997, I had found a publisher, and in May of 1998, it rolled out of the printing press and into stores. While the momentum was going, I worked diligently on my next title, *The Gods Who Walk Among Us*, an expository work focusing on the modern mystical resurrection of ancient gods into our society, and it was published in October of the same year. These two works together ignited a lot of discussion. New Agers were offended (understandably), and many conservative Christian leaders were shocked by my decision to focus on such unconventional theological spheres. I had expected this kind of reaction, so I was undeterred. However, to my surprise, feedback poured into my office from pastors around the nation who themselves had felt the need to address these categories of theology. As a result, I created teacher's guides and study guides following the material covered in both books and recruited my sheetrock-dusted family to collate them with a binding machine. I mailed these guides at a low cost to ministers all over the country to help them teach about these subjects in their home churches.

In the meantime, the "sea of unnumbered people" vision that Nita had seen during the Canaan Gospel Singers' prayer session started taking on a different shape. In her mind's eye that night so many years earlier, I had been on a stage in front of a crowd of people as big as the ocean. The throngs stretched so far away from me that no PA system in the world would ever blare loud enough for the whole congregation to hear, nor was there a speaking venue that could house masses of that size. But, as Nita and I had come to understand by this time in our ministry, God often quickens thoughts and visions in His people that fit the pictures their imaginations are capable of connecting to at that time. Back in the 1970s and early 1980s, only a few televangelists were reaching multitudes over the media. The Internet was not a part of every household, and the idea of book publishing wasn't one we would have placed any stock in since I didn't see myself as a gifted writer. Therefore, then, if Nita had closed her eyes and seen me on a platform in front of a gathering that would have been impossible (outside of a miracle as the only explanation), might that vision have been pointing to a day when numbers like these were reachable through means beyond my underdeveloped comprehension? Might God have used imagery that we were familiar with at the time to alert us of a coming day when things that didn't really exist yet would surface for us in the future? Ideas such as webisodes, blogsites, electronic publishing, online news outlets, video editing software, and social networking sites rife with promotional tools—*none* of these could have been in our thoughts when Nita had pointed her finger at me that night so long ago. Yet, it was now happening all around us, and even though in the 1990s, enterprises like YouTube, Netflix, Roku, and streaming from a "smart TV" in the living room had not yet been implemented in American homes, I knew that was where our world was headed.

As I was watching this world develop, as I was observing the inside workings of paperback trade publishing, I was starting to connect the dots from old-school book industry to the coming new world of media. Through technology, a sea of unnumbered people *could* be reached by our ministries, should the Lord continue to use me in this way.

Some visions create an overnight hype that fizzles almost immediately. A person sees or hears something, or a self-proclaimed prophet pours words over someone at a church service, and he or she celebrates what God has revealed, rushing out to take giant steps in the direction the prophet suggested. However, in many of these cases, the "revelation" loses momentum a week later, the dream dies, and the person on the receiving end of the spark loses interest and chalks it all up to a misunderstanding (or worse, he or she assumes that God fail to keep His promises). For Nita and me, it worked the opposite way: She saw something that would have been impossible that, at best, launched great confusion, but she believed in it *so much* that nothing could convince her otherwise over the years. I didn't have a big reaction to her vision, and did nothing differently in my daily life as an attempt to force what she had seen into fruition.

But…as the years rolled by, and as I saw the world changing around me to create the exact environment necessary to reach—with *one* voice— a *sea of people*, I began to believe Nita's vision more than I did the day she shared it with me. Thus, it was more important now than ever to channel myself into spreading the Gospel to those who were not being reached through traditional means, despite the fact that subjects such as "ancient gods" and "aliens" were throwing me into "the fringe."

As a result of my determination, I worked long hours while off the clock to write every chance I could, and I accepted every invitation for radio and television spots that I was offered. Before long, I launched an online Christian news site called Raiders News Update, where I published daily articles regarding biblical prophecy and its connection to modern global events. I tackled science and its relation to what humanity may become under the scalpel of robotic/human biological integration. I blared bold headlines concerning irreversible human/animal germline DNA tampering and what that means for tomorrow's generation. I addressed the enigmatic verses in Genesis 6 referring to a time when the "Sons of God" intermarried with human women and produced hybrid giant-offspring known as the "men of renown" just prior to the Flood in the days of Noah, and linked those biblical warnings to contemporary bloodline-altering agendas within the world's most reputable labs. I wrote about portals, gateways, and doorways between dimensions—whether they be physical or spiritual. There wasn't a single subject I refused to tackle if I thought—as was *always* my motive—that even one person might happen upon my articles as a result of more secular research into the paranormal or supernatural phenomena and follow my trails of theology connecting God and the mysteries of the universe and science. If even one soul came to rest in knowing that the God of the Bible has *everything* to do with these unconventional and peripheral subjects that aren't mentioned in mainstream church services, then I could rejoice knowing that He was once again relevant in the heart of someone who may never have come to Him otherwise.

If the boy from El Mirage, that lonely youth under the vast stars in a secluded corner of the desert, could grow up and turn his uncomfortable questions into spiritually thirst-quenching answers for the lost, then everything Nita said she saw might—*just might*—mean more as my lifelong calling than I thought. And as the counters on my news site were showing, a lot more than just one soul was listening to what the boy from El Mirage had to say…

The word was getting out, and quickly. Thomas Horn, the preacher, was talking about space aliens! Thomas Horn, the conservative, was discussing how today's modern America was embracing the gods of the ancient world! Thomas Horn, the family guy, was going off the deep end in expositions of Nephilim/Flood/Days of Noah theories that provoked the Church's longstanding and traditional Old Testament surveys!

But to the minority groups who had previously assumed the Bible was otherwise silent on such categories, Thomas Horn, the "visionary" (their words, not mine), was "finding answers."

From remodel to remodel, whenever I had an open hour in my busy schedule, I was receiving invitations to speak about my books on radio, and although my name was shrouded in controversy (even secular, sensational supermarket tabloids ran stories on me, twisting everything I said to sound as if I were a total crackpot), I was building a new ministry—the likes of which had a following that was growing rapidly.

The church organization Nita and I had served under for a number of years stood largely in support of my most recent endeavors. There were, of course, some who questioned why I left the pulpit in exchange for an irregular and eccentric ministry, but when given the opportunity to enlighten them, they usually endorsed my message. My intention was to reach *everyone*, including those who teetered on the balance of unbelief due to sensational and supernatural experiences. So, on the whole, our relationship with the organization remained intact. Nita had been serving as the Oregon state supervisor over the young girls' branch of the women's ministries department, so we were present at the state headquarters building for meetings fairly often. As casual conversation trails led to our current undertakings, they casually kept up with what I was doing outside the church as well, and knew that I had experience in construction.

Because headquarters were stationed at the entrance to the CCM (Camp and Conference Ministries) park where huge, annual camp meetings were held, I assisted in the remodeling of various buildings around the grounds. The conference center located in the middle of the park was in good shape, but the bathrooms were in great need of updating, so I jumped in to help. This led to other opportunities for me to use my construction skills on the same land, and I lent a hand in raising VIP cabins on the other side of the field. Then, the RV park bathrooms on the outskirts of the campus began to show signs of wear, so I helped renovate them as well. Then the tabernacle, then the tabernacle bathrooms, then the bunk beds in many of the buildings...

By this time, I had become a general contractor for the district, but this particular lot of land was now functioning very well, so I had started keeping an open mind about where God might lead me next.

Just after the turn of the century, when the nation was calming down after the height of the Y2K scare, I was approached by the Oregon district to consider taking a position as the executive director of the CCM board. I gave lots of thought to this offer, knowing that it placed me in a supervisory position over Camp Davidson, the youth camp located in the Sisters Mountains. The youth camp was in major disrepair: the central buildings were breaking down, the sewage was backing up, the cabins were falling apart, and the grounds were rough and overgrown from years of neglect. It wasn't the fault of the hardworking staff the camp had employed in years prior, because they had worked like bees trying to keep the place maintained. However, the camp only operated at full capacity during the summer months and a few weeks in winter, when construction was not an option since hundreds of campers were using the facilities, and the rest of the year it didn't draw enough revenue to keep a full staff. Therefore, in the off-seasons, the harsh weather patterns of the mountain would wreak havoc on the campground, and there simply weren't enough people there to see to the proper reparations. What the district needed then, they said, was a camp director who could remain on-site, year-round, one who had experience in construction and who could see to the repairs of the land in between camp groups or whenever the schedule permitted a remodel. As executive director of the CCM board, I was required to live on the premises, which essentially meant that I would be fulfilling the role of camp director during my tenure.

I was told I didn't have to give an immediate answer. I could go home, pray about it, and get back to them. On my end, however, my answer arrived before their proposal ever did. I was tired of construction and wanted to focus on writing. Radio opportunities were soaring, and there were hungry people who needed the truth of the Word.

"I've decided I'm not going to Camp Davidson," I told Nita almost immediately following their proposition. "I understand why they would ask me, but it's not my ministry."

"Just like that?" she asked, tilting her head to one side.

I shook my head, confused. "What do you mean? You think we should go?" She had given me every reason to believe that a lifetime of continual drywall-mud-glops was not her sincerest heart's desire.

"I don't know if we should or shouldn't yet. But, aren't you going to pray about it?"

I considered her question. It was a valid one, but my mind was set. "I don't need to pray about something I know is clearly not what the Lord has called me to do," I said, feeling smart about my deduction.

"You mean," she said with her eyebrows knitted together, "you aren't even going to *pray about it?*"

Nita's rebuttal hadn't challenged me directly, as she hadn't countered my intellectual breakdown of the situation. Instead, however, she had appealed to my duty of obedience to Divine authority, and that was a challenge I couldn't ignore. I thought of every excuse I could, but quickly each one returned void in contrast to a servant's willingness to obey his Master's potential order.

"Ugh… Fine, I'll pray about it."

And I did.

And I didn't like my answer.

Over the next several weeks, each time I bowed my head and asked for the Lord's direction where this "Camp Davidson" assignment was concerned, I heard that same still, small voice prompting me to open my mind beyond the box of "Tom's thoughts and conclusions." What in the *world* did a CCM director position have to do with where God had been taking *me*? It wouldn't be complementary to the work I had been doing for the Kingdom; in fact, it would be an unequivocal distraction from it. I knew that I knew that I knew I was on the right track with my writing, and now I found myself praying about a campground?

A *campground?!*

And the Holy Spirit was telling me to consider it?!

And my wife—the same wife who had the vision of the sea of people, which had nothing to do with camping—was open to the idea?!

I didn't want to think I had more lessons to learn on my journey to becoming the author or radio personality I knew I could be, but I couldn't ignore that all signs were pointing to go to Camp Davidson in obedience to a call I couldn't wrap my brain around yet. Eventually, I reluctantly agreed to a one-year contract. God had taken me to Cornerstone in Crescent City against my heartfelt pleas to the otherwise, and not only had I spent some of the happiest years of my life there, but my concepts of ministry had been reformed through experiences on radio and television. I had chosen after that to put away childish things and fully trust in the Lord. So, as much as I didn't want to do it, if I was being *called* to the camp...I was *going* to the camp. Enough said.

I gave the district my decision shortly after this conclusion had stamped itself in my psyche, knowing that if God wanted me to put writing and radio aside, there was a reason. A lesson to be learned.

And *oh* the lesson!...

It was the greatest of them all.

God knew that I had to see my family—my *whole* family, not just Nita and me—at work in ministry for what He ultimately had planned for me, for Nita, for my kids, and for that sea...

My youngest daughter, Donna, had already worked at the youth camp for one winter and one summer as a seasonal staff member when she was sixteen, and my son, Joe, had taken a job there as a recreational facilitator at twenty. So when Nita and I took on our one-year commitment, it seemed natural to keep the two of them on as permanent staff. Together, we would see to the needs of the campers when they were present, and we would remodel the grounds when they were gone.

I had no idea of what I was getting into when I agreed to take on the role of CCM director. When we arrived, it appeared as if every window, every wall, every pipe, every heater, even every shrub was broken or decrepit in one way or another. I knew that funding was an issue, so I started making calls. One of the first donation groups I brought out to the grounds was from the Ford Foundation. Two men followed me around with clipboards and cell phones while I showed them all that needed to be fixed. I treated them to a decent lunch from the cafeteria and we talked about the possibilities of a grant. In the end, however, they were both convinced that the camp was in such dire circumstances that it was too high a financial risk. If they agreed to pour funds into this place and then the project was abandoned when the workers became exhausted, it would all be a waste. However, as a gracious, last-word compromise (that I'm sure they didn't believe I would make good on), one of the men said, "Tom, call us again in a year. If you have made significant progress, we will reconsider a grant from the Ford Foundation to help you all out."

During that year, I drew from whatever crevices of the budget I could find, made appeals to as many donors as I could, and worked my hands to the bone. Joe, Donna, and Nita also worked continuously, frequently reporting fifteen-hour days, six days a week. We hired a maintenance man and food-service personnel, and brought out volunteers to help with labor. As each person was brought to the camp, he or she was told in no uncertain terms that the job description would be diverse. When the camp was facilitating large groups, we would serve as everything from cooks and recreational staff to hosts and toilet cleaners. When the campers were gone, we would be painters, planters, landscapers, builders, trench-diggers, and old-sink-ripper-outers, among a number of other titles. Wherever intense work was underway, it was an all-hands-on-deck labor force until we could put another checkmark on the list of the many necessary and extreme facility overhauls.

Whereas we never expected anyone to work more hours in a day than were on the work schedule (this was never expected of family members, either), we quickly found that almost everyone who came to help was willing to keep at it for long, strenuous hours if it meant contributing to the Kingdom of God. We were blessed by the giving nature of men and women who put the needs of the campgrounds above their own as a ministry to the Lord, a labor of love for the lost, as it were. Although we probably maxed out at around ten people that first year on average, our crew accomplished enough that one would have thought we had employed fifty muscle men around the clock for months on end.

It was a miracle what we were able to do with such a tight budget. Before I had been there for a full twelve months, the cabins, cabin bathrooms, kitchens, dormitories, and many other small facilities were all completely gutted and rebuilt, and those that were not finished were well on their way. The septic system was replaced with brand-new tanks, the plumbing lines rerouted for efficiency, and the electric wiring was updated to code. When the final touches such as fresh paint and décor had been applied throughout the camp, personal of those coming through the grounds were shaking their heads in wonder. People who had camped there for years didn't recognize the place, and feedback was unanimously positive from all sides.

When the men from the Ford Foundation returned the next summer, they were astounded.

"Tom, you achieved absolutely every little thing you promised to do, and then went well beyond that. I have to admit, I'm really shocked to see all this."

"Well," I said, shaking my head, "I didn't do it alone by any stretch of the imagination. These folks here have been working their tails off without stopping. They get up early, sweat all day, go to bed late, and do it all again the next day. We all take Sunday off, but that's just about the only time I can convince them to rest, because each of them are treating this like their own ministry. They've really taken this place personally, you know. Under their wings, so to speak."

"It shows. It shows, Tom. This camp ain't even the same place."

"So I hear."

After another lunch at the cafeteria, the men from Ford pulled out their clipboards and took notes while we talked. I could tell that I was closer to getting a grant, but the grounds still had many eyesores. The pool needed to be completely redone because it had structural damage as a result of an avalanche years prior, and *this* time it needed to be permanently protected from future ground-warming landslides. That would cost a pretty penny. The mini-golf course's rickety platforms and walkways not only debilitated the golfers' aim—thereby canceling out the purpose of the game entirely—but they were a safety hazard to the players, who had been seen on more than one occasion tripping over a jutting board and toppling downhill. The motel-like hall that sat atop the hill next to the food-service director's cabin had been in better shape than the rest of the buildings when we arrived, but now, in contrast to the other updates, it appeared broken-down and crumbling. The main office was located in the worst possible spot in all the camp, just outside the dining hall, where our administrative staff was constantly derailed by curious campers who wanted to ask questions about their church programs our staff wouldn't have the answers to anyway. It would need to be moved, and that would require a major upgrade to an unused building up the hill. And the chapel! I was embarrassed even showing the men from Ford where the campers held their services. The floor was splintered wood, sagging in several places and threatening to fall through, and there were no bathrooms. (At night, the campers had to trek through the trees to the cabin bathrooms, and this also presented a safety issue during the icy, slippery months.) Not to mention that the chapel was a tight fit for our larger groups anyway, sometimes leading to standing-room-only services, which were distracting to worshipers. In my opinion, the chapel needed to be completely torn down. In its place, I had blueprints for a grand lodge that would not only meet the needs of all services, but it would have two large indoor bathrooms, an indoor snack shack (our current one was outside the chapel and, yes, you guessed it, it was falling apart), and it would double as a new recreational facility with an indoor skate park and rock-climbing wall.

These were big plans for a campground that had so little income. Though I also had visions of a future date when the camp would be bursting with groups booked back to back all year round—generating a revenue for the organization that this site had never provided and therefore justifying the amount of money I was asking for—a vision was all I had. There was not yet any solid proof that what we were hoping to build would even bring in the numbers I planned on. Despite all my grand ideas, there still was an element of risk. I couldn't blame the men from Ford for not giving me an immediate answer.

"Well, Tom, this is all really impressive. We've got your grant application and we've seen all you've done here, and all you plan to do. I know we sure would like to help you, but we're gonna need to get back to headquarters and discuss it further with the powers that be out in Roseburg, you know?"

"Oh sure, sure. I understand completely," I said with a cordial smile as the three of us stood.

"We'll give you call soon and see if there's anything we can do."

One of the men held his hand out to shake mine, but I didn't take it. Instead, I stared at his hand a moment and then slowly lifted my gaze back to the clipboard at his chest.

"Hang on," I said, blinking. "Did you say *Roseburg*?"

"Yeah, that's where our office is at."

I furrowed my brow for a moment in thought. I crossed my arms over my chest and connected the dots…

Ford…

Roseburg…

"Are you guys talking about *Pappy Ford*?" I asked.

Immediately their eyes grew wide and their brows lifted in surprise. The men shared a glance and then smiled.

"You *knew* Pappy?"

I explained to them that I had spoken with Pappy years prior when I was the pastor of Tenmile, and that he and I had already discussed a grant for a new church—which he appeared to be on board with when I left the materials in reliable hands and moved on in my ministry. The men from Ford had a good laugh at our ironic discovery, and then informed me that *only* family, close friends, and people he trusted ever knew him as "Pappy."

And that was it. I never made the story out to be more than it was. I let them know honestly that I had only spoken with him one time over the phone. I never invented some tale about having shared golf-swing tips or hunting trip stories or sending chocolates on his birthday, but I didn't have to. These men were convinced that just by knowing him as "Pappy," I had gained his trust. Having somehow unintentionally invoked the authority of Pappy's name posthumously, it was only a matter of paperwork.

"If Pappy can build you a church, then *we* can build you a camp. Right?"

God had provided yet again, and the wheels He set in motion for this provision had been turning for over twenty years.

Between the enormously generous approval from the Ford Foundation, the grant I obtained from the Murdock Foundation, and several other strings I found to pull with the district's support, money was coming in from everywhere. That one-year commitment at Camp Davidson became a total of seven years in Camp and Conference Ministries.

During the first few years, my eldest daughter, Allie, was able to quit her job and come join us as well, so I now had all five of my immediate family—including a few grandkids—in one place again.

Season after season, our family and camp staff poured blood, sweat, and tears into giving that campground a complete revamp. When we weren't working on a remodel, we were diligently advertising to groups outside the organization, and slowly but surely, our calendar started filling up. Some of the more prestigious groups had a policy that they would only stay at facilities that had achieved American Camping Association (ACA) accreditation, so for at least a full year, our staff redesigned grounds policies, safety procedures, and emergency response systems to meet that criteria. When the ACA came to inspect our changes, they, like the men from Ford, were astounded at all we had been able to implement in one year, and we found ourselves ACA approved within the week. As a result, the door was opened for additional groups to visit our site, and the revenue was rising.

After most of the remodeling was complete, a lot of my attention turned to making the grounds aesthetically beautiful. One particular couple, Arthur and Virginia, had lived in their RV on the back of the grounds from the time we started working there. Because they were elderly and needed a break from all the contruction labor, and because they loved nature and wildlife, they were thrilled when I asked if they would like to help me with landscaping. Leaves and branches had fallen from the thick woods around the camp for a good fifty years or so without ever being completely cleared. Although the main walkways were clear for the campers to move about, just on the other side of all the pretty red fences were heaps of pine needles, maple leaves, and bits of wood accumulating to almost a foot high. For two summers straight, Arthur and Virginia took to the trees with rakes and shovels and garbage bags, lifting and hoisting debris and cleaning up the flora. This project the last item on my list of priorities, but the timing of the removal of this eyesore couldn't have been better.

In 2003, after routine thunderstorms passed over our area, we quickly received word that a tree had been struck by lightning and a forest fire was rapidly spreading in the 90-degree weather. Camp Davidson, as well as all other surrounding campsites, were under strict and immediate evacuation notice. Joe and Allie instantly but calmly activated all the ACA emergency response methods (Donna was off that day and already in Bend, Oregon), and almost four hundred people—including staff, volunteers, counselors, and campers—were evacuated to the nearby city of Sisters in less than two hours. We were not allowed to go back for several weeks while the firefighters fought back the raging forest infernos. The fire destroyed *miles* of land, including nearby facilities like ours. However, thanks to Arthur and Virginia for their scraping the debris and undergrown down to the very soil for aesthetic purposes, and thanks to God for His ever-present watchfulness, the flames went in a loop right around Camp Davidson without scorching a single tree. The aerial shots of the fires were incredible. It looked as though a protective bubble followed our exact property lines, the other side of which was smoking ruination. In fact, the firefighters took one look at the clean, debris-free grounds and decided that our camp would be their refuge for the duration of the fires. When we finally did return home, we discovered that the firefighters had thanked us for the use of our sleeping facilities by cleaning the four hundred plates of half-eaten food that had been left during lunch the day of of the sudden evacuation.

Had Arthur and Virginia not cleared the leaves and branches, our grounds would have been ripe for brushfire. Had we not just freshly implemented emergency evacuation procedures to meet ACA accreditation requirements, we would have been running around in a panic when the evacuation notice came to camp.

As so many other pastors have said throughout the years: God may be early, but He's never late, and He *always* provides. That just never stops being true.

Our days as a family in the camping ministry were eventful, that's for sure. Many of us recall them as a long, five- to seven-year blur of activity. And we eventually did all that we promised to do, including raising several new buildings and a grand lodge, and eventually increasing our year-round business. By the time we left, there weren't three unbooked weeks in a calendar year, and Camp Davidson had become a safe place for all ages to visit.

However, probably the singular most important part of this era in my life has yet to be told. It wasn't just what my family and I did for the Lord in those days, but irrefutably what the Lord did for our family. By our third year there, all of us were working together in ways we couldn't have foreseen. I was the CCM executive director and Nita was the head of administration. Our eldest, Allie, had become a crucial multidepartmental secretary, running all over the place to make all of the workings of a camp function. Not one department could flow effectively without her. Joe and his wife, Katherine, had become the recreation department heads: They trained our lifeguards; maintained the pool chemicals; taught the campers safety rules at our high-ropes challenge course and zip lines; and supervised all other leisure activities like bike riding, paddleboating, and other water sports at the lake. Donna was our head chef; supervisor over seasonal youth staff, which often numbered upwards of thirty teenagers; and supervisor of custodial duties between departing and incoming groups.

Just like when we first arrived and our job descriptions had been diverse, we melded together as a family and continued that pattern. Each of us was trained to function as a leader in every *other* department. Joe and Katherine might have been testing the PH balance of the pool water when a group was leaving, but they were never above scrubbing toilets and showers when the camp had to be cleaned from top to bottom during the four hours before the next busloads. Donna might have been an expert behind the spice rack, but after lunch was cleaned up, with dinner was three hours away and fifty campers threatening to dive in the shallow end of the pool, she was always willing to don some sunscreen and a whistle to lifeguard a swim session. Nita might have been taking phone calls, organizing incoming groups, and signing checks, but when another body was needed at the belay post to keep our climbing campers safely harnessed, she was right there. Allie may have been everywhere at once, but when a meal was being served and three hundred people were asking for more eggs, she was a proficient scrambler.

We leaned each on the other for everything, and not only did this bring us closer than we ever thought we could be, but we realized that even in distinct and separate departments of ministry, the trust we had for one another was unquestionable and solid. And this would play a *huge part* in the ministries yet to come…

We also got to know each other's heart's desires intimately, and a camaraderie unrelated to camping ministry began to thread together as each of us realized that our own talents complemented the others in unexpected ways.

As a child, Joe had always been "in character." His imagination was wild—twenty-four hours a day, seven days a week, without a break. He often created characters that he would slip into throughout the day just to be silly. With each one he intermittently played, he would take on this other voice and way of speaking. Today's child psychologists would probably have a heyday analyzing him and trying to diagnose away the creativity, but when he was little, people just saw it for what it was: ingenuity. To name just a short list of his characters, there was "Joebo," a play on Rambo; Dr. Joekyll, a play on Dr. Jekyll; "Danny," a shy teenager who didn't want to eat his veggies; "the umpire," a man who ran around randomly yelling "yer out!"; "the jaw," a young, sly, and mischievous character who talked with his lower jaw jutting out; "Grampa Sam," an old man who complained about everything in a thick, Southern accent; and so, *so* many more. He had a lot of fun surprising us all the time with new personalities he would try on and take off like sweater vests. Everyone who observed Joe in action had the same reaction: "That kid is gonna be an actor!"

From the first time Joe ever set eyes on a guitar as a toddler, he was enamored with the instrument. His very first song was "I See, I Saw," and those were the lyrics, in their entirety, for a full seven minutes. A woman in church once told him, "I bet you're gonna be really good at that guitar someday when you learn to play," and his answer inspired a hearty chuckle: "I *already* know how to play the guitar. I just have to learn the chords." As soon as we could afford to buy him one of his own, Joe surprised me and Nita when he spent hours on end away from the world in his room just plucking, strumming, and fingering the neck of that thing until there wasn't a Gospel song in existence that he couldn't master well before he knew how to read and write. He wrote many original songs as well, almost all of them Christian, until he was old enough to develop a steady sense of humor. *Then* an era of the most hilarious tunes ever heard came through one of Joe's many alternate personalities he affectionately named "Mans 'n Me." (We never did get an explanation as to why Joe felt the need to live "in character" most of his childhood, or why his alternates would have such bizarre names, but we later discovered God's use for such creativity…)

Allie and Donna were both Broadway musical fanatics from the moment they left the womb. As such, they may have taken on roles of actual characters defined by Hollywood or off of an original London cast live recording somewhere instead of originals like Joe, but they, too, were frequently slipping in and out of character. After years of their own practice, both of them had learned how to mimic various dramatic styles. From Doris Day's innocent, prancing, golden-girl grace notes, to Christin Daaé's high shrills in *The Phantom of the Opera*, and the crafty, dirt-smeared, cockney spatterings of the Artful Dodger in *Oliver* to the loud, boisterous, and heart-on-the-floor belting of Grizabella's "Memories" from *Cats*, there just wasn't a character these girls couldn't portray *and* sing with proficient execution…and oftentimes *with real tears!* Before Allie or Donna either one could speak a full sentence of their own design, they were both singing entire songs with the words completely memorized. Additionally, both girls were writers and painters, and had a flare for anything craft-related.

Allie had always had a knack for taking a complete organizational nightmare and whipping it into a flowing, graceful system.

And Donna, from her youngest age I can remember, seemed to have a pencil surgically attached to her fingers; many, *many* fantastically written poems, articles, small stage scripts, and novellas came out of her in her youth.

While at Camp Davidson, these talents did occasionally produce entertaining skits or mini-musicals at a company party or weekend staff retreat (that Allie expertly organized), what we *really* discovered was how each of us, and mostly my kids, played off of each other's talents and interests as a result of being in such close proximity. What they created in those moments were the earliest forms of what we would do in later ministries. And had we not come to Camp Davidson as a family, we may never have known how well we work together in a professional setting as well as how our talents and interests complement each other's for use in the Kingdom. I may have continued writing on my own, and the kids may have gone on to pursue unrelated careers or ministries. Together at camp, though, we melded into a unit that would carry us well beyond paddleboats and scrambled eggs.

In the midst of hectic workdays, hundreds of campers looking for hot cocoa and stomping fresh melty-snow puddles all over the dining room was no big thing, because Joe would slip into his adult alternate personality, "Big H," and sing some ridiculous impromptu song about cocoa and snow puddles, and Allie and Donna would back him up in perfect harmony, mysteriously guessing in advance what his next words were going to be. In the kitchens, in front of fifteen stressed-out teenage summer staffers, Donna would burst into a heartfelt song about tomato soup and butter, Joe would run over and "beatbox" behind her, creating some weird, hip-hip/rock-opera ensemble, and Nita would hear it from the other room and rush in to provide an a cappella bass riff. Allie would observe a safety rule being broken for the umpteenth time in one day, and rather than cry about it, she would lift her hands and begin a sarcastically emotional monologue, playing off of Donna's sudden entrance as another "character," and then Joe would enter "the show" to contribute his nonsense before they all gave a bow and exited "stage right" (wherever that was at the moment).

I have heard it said on more than one occasion by different people and at different times that if our family, during our time at Camp Davidson, had been followed around by a live camera crew, we could have been the next hit reality TV show.

But it was more, *far* more, than just a survival instinct to channel laughter through odd means when crying was the alternative. Our family saw over and over again how harmoniously we worked together, each borrowing strength from the other when our own was tapped dry. The situation was so unique because we were a family both at work and off the clock, and unless a person has lived at a campground miles away from civilization for the better half of a decade, it is hard to explain the isolation that can materialize in such circumstances. The stress that can occur in front of a backdrop like this often sets off bickering, bringing out the worst in people. Seeing too much of one face all the time—even a brother, sister, mother, father, spouse, son, or daughter—when everyone is running around like chickens with missing heads can lead to extreme annoyance. One might start to notice little things about others around them that eventually creates an antagonistic environment. The pressure cooker we lived in was overwhelming, and just when we thought the heat couldn't get any higher, some unforeseen episode would come along and crank it up to well past boiling. We saw this manifesting on many occasions between others on our staff. Between us, however, gossip, glares, disapproving side glances, and petty squabbles were nonexistent.

This is not to say that we were perfect, or that we never had a moment of weakness when our internal feelings showed through the professional exterior we attempted to always model. It *is* to say that when that occurred, it was never once—*never once*—against each other, and drama amidst family was simply not an issue. After long, hard days of frenzy, we still had barbecues and holidays and dinners and family nights wherein we only ever approached each other with joyous anticipation of one another's company.

We were a core team. We all learned how to be leaders in our own departments, and still submit to those leading other departments, even if it was the same kid sister one grew up yanking pigtails at the breakfast table with.

We wrote policy together. We fixed what was broken together. We developed new efficiency techniques together. We learned how to drum up revenue together. We handled crisis after crisis together.

We built an entire ministry…*together.*

And it was just the beginning.

Those *same skills* that we learned to sharpen as a family unit are what we have to draw from in our bailiwick now, years later, with all we're currently doing in service to the Lord…

When everything that could be done at camp was done, we once again passed the reins to the next minister and packed our bags for what would likely be our final ministerial move.

For a very brief period back in the Portland, Oregon, area, Nita and I had invested in a small business while I wrote, Donna got married, and we all waited for the next clear calling. It came quickly. Exhausted by all the taxes and increasing lifestyle concerns that plagued the West Coast, we all simultaneously felt the need to radically relocate: not just to another city, but to another state entirely. After a lot of research, we felt that Missouri held the greatest promise for new beginnings. Nita, my kids, and I all set sails for the "Show-Me State" shortly thereafter.

Once we settled into our new homes in middle America, I had another book hot off the press: *Nephilim Stargates*. My kids landed jobs that were unrelated to anything I was doing for about a year. Donna worked as a contract processor for a timeshares company in Branson; Allie became the food-service director for a school district near West Plains, Missouri, and Joe ran a guitar shop. All were busy doing what they had to do to bring home a check, but before long, the interest generated through my writing was creating more work than Nita and I could handle alone.

Just before the move, I had started an online survival products store that until this point had been a small task to supervise. Now, however, running SurvivorMall.com required a least two or three full-time workers. During my time at Camp Davidson, I had made several significant connections within the industry of books, and I was now launching my own publishing company and all that entails (editing, proofreading, typesetting, design, promotion, etc.) so that I could be in full control of all that I wrote and the royalties those titles drew. I hired staff to assist me in the creation and design of my titles, but they were all remote, working from their computers hundreds or thousands of miles away, so everything that had to happen at the company office had to be accomplished by Nita or myself. The first of two publishing companies I created appealed to the mainstream audience, and as mentioned prior, I wasn't a mainstream minister. Therefore, I sold that company and started another one that focused directly on biblical expositions of prophecy, science, the supernatural, the paranormal, and the official disclosure of disturbing international current events. This second company was named Defender Publishing (which is thriving to this day).

As if this isn't an overwhelming list of endeavors, I also presented a radio show several times a week, appeared in occasional television spots, and regularly spoke at conferences with a schedule that was increasingly filling up my calendar.

So, as the budget allowed, I eventually brought each of my kids—and their spouses—to work with me again (although, just as before, Allie was a few years behind Joe and Donna). The family unit was as it had been in Oregon, each department functioning with the full respect and cooperation of all others, and every department head wearing at least ten hats at any point. Donna was my personal secretary for the publishing company, full-time editor, full-time proofreader, and production manager. Joe was the entire customer service department for Survivor-Mall.com, manager over the shipping warehouse, and the filler of almost every online order. Whenever I advertised a large sale through my store, everyone, including Nita, was in the packing room, and nobody was "too good" to slap labels on hundreds or thousands of boxes to fulfill the highest priority needs. Whenever I needed to attend a major conference, it was, as always, an all-hands-on-deck labor force working behind the scenes to pack up the books and work the sales counter in the hallways of the venue. When one person in the family couldn't make it alone in his or her department, the others fled to their assistance and chipped in to keep things moving.

It was absolutely identical to our time in camping ministry in every sense, except for the literal functions of the jobs, themselves. Although Allie wasn't working for me just yet, she drove down to help any way she could when she was available on weeknights and weekends. Whenever I held a promotional sale for survival products, impromptu monologues were the brainchild of my kids while they built home and car survival kits. With eight thousand piling orders for another book title, mini-musicals in perfect harmony materialized above the din of shipping-tape guns in the warehouse instead of cries of stress and anguish. When the production schedule had fifteen books all being released at the next International Christian Retail Show by a multitude of authors in our circle, beatboxing hip-hop/rock-operas were the norm while the back of our Chevy Trailblazer was being packed beyond recommended capacity.

It was camp all over again, just as we had learned in those days while God was sharpening my ministry skills, just as God had intended for us to learn. And it was the greatest lesson of all our lives combined.

But something else unrelated to workplace entertainment began to form around this time. Yes, every member of my family was capable of running departments of this new ministry. Yes, every member of my family was capable of full trust in one another during work hours and still cherishing each other's company afterward. Yes, every member of my family was capable of being both professional and fun-loving, *and* knowing the different times when each of those behaviors were most appropriate.

However, every member of my family began to shine in his and her own different but complementary ways that I never even knew my ministry would need, and much of it was relating to who they were as children growing up.

When I needed a promotional video for my next two books, *Apollyon Rising* and *Forbidden Gates*, Joe used the recording equipment that he had familiarized himself with through his music, went into character, and performed the voiceovers for (and sometimes the characters on film *within*) the advertisement. The knowledge he had regarding moods in melodies was already at top-notch level without any training, and the score ambiance of the promos was incredibly professional. Donna's addiction to theatrics had given her a head start on knowing what needed to be seen and how dramatically it needed to be executed in order to convey a powerful and drawing visual message within just a few minutes. Her days experimenting with video editing software for camp projects allowed her to jump in without any training as well. The two of them produced marketing ads that immediately drew a slew of emails to my account. *Everyone* wanted to know what company I had hired to produce such incredible commercials!

The company nearly exploded out of control with international attention when I released *Petrus Romanus: The Final Pope Is Here.* (This book, also, had an incredible promotional video created by Joe and

Donna.) I remain convinced today that much of the inspiration of that book came from revelations that were given to me by God the night I passed away in bed next to my wife years prior. However, as you are about to read, I am still, as we speak, seeing the depth of the revelations God showed me that night.

And it is *all* about my family and the ministries God has moved us in place to carry out.

Eventually, when we grew to the point that we could no longer continue to function without the ultimate organizer, Allie agreed to come on board. Since the day her presence graced the scene, every single department has melded to flow more professionally together as a whole unit. Her creativity has inspired projects we wouldn't have even known how to tackle, and through her, all distribution and electronic publishing channels began running elegantly.

And, now that I had all the right people in all the right places, and my publishing business model through Defender Publishing was nailed down, I was equipped for blastoff in the paramount ministry God had prepared us all for: SkyWatch Television.

All this alone would have been more than the boy from El Mirage could have dreamed up had I been limited merely to my own imagination. But what we are doing *now*, *today*, trumps all of this together, and there are winds blowing in and throughout our work that are still so recent that even I, the leader of the entire entourage, cannot explain…

I believe that a revival is on the horizon for our country, and probably for the world. I have watched as the global faith-drought and bombarding daily social schisms have paved the way for a worldwide reaction. It appears that today *everyone* is starving for something real, something deep, something that truly feeds our innate hunger for spiritual satisfaction.

When we log online to casually check our social networking accounts, we are flooded with political memes, public opinion, harsh words by "Internet trolls," and rights activism from hostilely opposing lifestyle groups. When we drive to work, the radio blasts us with new stories of turmoil on foreign soil and the safety threats that poses to our friends, neighbors, spouses, and children. When we attend church, our pastors address the latest list of reasons we need to stand up and fight against the enemy's spiritual attacks upon our country. Everywhere we look and every place we go, right now, today, people are feeling the weight of this invisible and demoralizing force.

Research into the history of every major revival or Great Awakening our world has witnessed suggests that all the factors that led to such fervent outbreaks are alive and well in every country on our planet as we speak. We are poised like a cornered canine by a ravaging, international beast that has terrorized us for decades, and when we lash back—if it is through passionate prayer, falling on our faces before the Almighty God, global repentance, and allowing God to be God in our lives and nations—we will experience a resuscitation of the Church body like nothing any previous generation has ever seen before.

I believe that a Great Awakening is just around the corner, and when it approaches, I want Defender Publishing and SkyWatch TV to be a part of it. And from the responses our ministries are receiving now, I have great reason to believe we already are.

There was a day I rested on the hot sands in Arizona and asked that mysterious Presence of the universe what my purpose on this earth would be. Without a single smidgen of doubt, I have my answer.

Never doubt yourself, no matter your age, race, gender, or self-perceived potential. You are a child of God, created in *His* image. Walk the path of life with confidence, knowing that this temporal realm we live in is just the beginning, knowing that every step you take in the Lord leaves an impression in the ground behind you that others will follow. More people than you know are aware of what you do with your time while you're here.

You have been formed and molded by the Master Potter. You may be the greatest tool in your generation hiding right now in plain sight, just waiting for the call on your life to descend upon you and explode outward to everyone around you. You may, on the inside, just be a little boy or girl from some small town outside of Nowheresville, looking at the sky and wondering what your life means, but when the Lord of the universe beckons…no enemy, no foe, *no devil in hell* can stop the power of the call upon an obedient child of God.

The Holy Spirit *knows you already*. He knows your heart, your desires, your purpose, and your potential.

He knows your *footprint*.

Go.

Conclusion

A few years before the time of this writing, God showed us He was taking my family and our ministries to a whole new level. I am now witnessing sides of Nita, Joe, Allie, and Donna that I wasn't aware existed.

I had given Donna writing projects before, but this one was different. In a private meeting with her, I started with what I believed at the time to be an approximate 250-page book idea. She wasn't going to write the whole thing, certainly not. But I needed at least a little help regarding the research.

"I've been thinking about redemption of the lost," I said. "Those who believe they are really, *really* lost. Unreachable. Bound for hell. No hope."

I watched as Donna nodded, flipped open her laptop, and clicked around for a fresh word document to take notes.

"In twenty-five years of pastoring, I met all kinds of people that thought they had committed unforgiveable acts of sin, and they no longer believed they were even *eligible* for salvation. Then, back in the mid-eighties, I got my hands on that book by that Manson Family killer, Susan Atkins. She had found God, or so she said. I need you to read that book and present me with a case to see if we could expound a little on that idea. Maybe we could add another person to the list as well, and come up with a title of our own. I think I remember Sean Sellers having a testimony like that also. I would like to help people understand that nothing they do, nothing they have ever done, will permanently separate a man, woman, or child from the far-reaching grace of God. It's kind of an, 'If there is hope for Susan Atkins, there is hope for me' idea. What do you think?"

Boy, that had done it. Donna's hands were clacking those laptop keys faster than I had ever seen. And she remained anything *but* silent. I had no idea that, as a teenager, my little bookworm had been reading book after book in that same genre. Within that single twenty-minute meeting, off the top of her head she named off the names of at least five other criminals whose stories were similar.

One week later, we had a follow-up meeting, and Donna nearly blew the coffee mug right out of my hands with the facts and figures she had compiled. She presented me with nearly twenty names of famous conversions and the incredible work she had done to outline all those stories made me immediately forego my first length estimate. She had already begun writing some terrific material on Susan Atkins. This was going to be a serious book, a real ministry tool, and perhaps the most important book I had ever published.

One by one, we discussed each of the case studies she had found for our project and we eventually narrowed the list down to seven stories of murderers whose conversions were so credible and transparent that we had what we needed to proceed. Who knew my little Broadway star was such a proficient researcher?! And who knew she could write like *that*, having only had a few classes in writing?

I leaned on her a lot during the writing of that book, and in November of 2014, *Redeemed Unredeemable* arrived from off the press. It is now in the hands of prisoners all over the nation, and we have received much feedback from readers including those behind bars who have informed us that our book has given them hope.

That, alone, is a reason to celebrate. Apart from statistics of this one title, however, is the fact that ever since its completion, Donna has been a full-time writer for our ministry. Her work has appeared in many books—not the least of which have included *Dead Pets Don't Lie*, *No Fences*, *When Once We Were a Nation*, and *God's Ghostbusters*. Her research was invaluable in *On the Path of the Immortals* as well as several other titles that are in production now, and she wrote the script to our two-Telly-award-winning documentary film *INHUMAN: The Final Phase of Man Is Here*. She is busy day in and day out using her writing skills to minister, and no matter what happens to me, Donna has a huge future in reaching the lost! This is, of course, heaped atop the fact that whenever I wish to write about something with the demanding schedule of seemingly a thousand jobs, I have someone who can gather the initial facts and outlines together so that my own writing is a better and more cohesive.

Joe set out several years ago to form a band called Joe Horn and Broken for Good. It is nowhere near his first band project, but I believe God has used all of Joe's experiences in his previous ventures to lead to a full anointing of this one. Nita is Joe's drummer, Allie is his keytarist, and Donna his countervocalist (backup vocals and lead female vocals). James, Donna's husband, is the bassist, and Stan, a very close family friend, is the rhythm guitarist. Joe, of course, is the lead male vocalist and lead guitarist, and both his and Donna's vocal sounds are unique due to their creative background and spontaneity. Altogether, this group produces a sound that is simply indescribable. For now, we are referring to it as "blues gospel," but that is a far reach from all of which it this group of musicians is capable. They don't sound like any other Christian band in the world, and everyone who hears their music agrees.

One song they have written is called "Jonny." Stan came up with the original chords, Joe expressed concept ideas for the song's purpose, and Donna wrote the lyrics while she was also working on the research for *Redeemed Unredeemable*. Not surprisingly, the song does not follow your average worship track. Contrarily, it begins by telling the dramatic story of a criminal who is running from the law, had cut all family ties, burned bridges, and made a complete mess out of his life. After being caught in a criminal act, Jonny is put in prison for a time, reflects on all the bad decisions he's made and, upon his release, decides to turn his life over to the Lord. His conversion is sincere and powerful. From there, Jonny takes the Gospel to all his oldest friends, repairs the family damage he created, and at the end of the song, he drives away on his motorcycle a changed man.

It was, in all ways, a musical complement to *Redeemed Unredeemable*. But apart from that is the way it speaks to each listener with a story of hope, right where a person stands, no matter what he or she has done.

When the song was recorded, Joe reached out to a long-standing pastor friend who agreed to play the role of Jonny in the music video, and when the filming was done, this friend felt led to record a short "Prodigal Son" sermon in our television studio. The result of this became a DVD ministry tool that is now being given free to every outlet we can dip into, and lives are being changed.

In addition to all of this, Joe has now launched the first youth-age ministry through SkyWatch Television. *Teens Rock* is in its beginning stages of reaching out to young people all over the world with televised Bible studies, addressing hard-hitting questions that teen crowds can relate to. His wife, Katherine, is hosting alongside him when she's not operating in her role as the head supervisor of the SkyWatch bookstore and shipping warehouse.

Allie has an unbelievable mind. It appears that there is very little she *can't* do. She sings, writes, paints, plays the keytar, and so many other things I am only just learning about. However, a few years ago, when our company took over our own book distribution to large buyers such as Ingram, Amazon, and Baker & Taylor, our entire company began to rely on her administrative abilities in such a crucial way that, without her, we may not have been able to keep the lights on. She is everyone's closest friend around the offices, but she is also a major part of every department's central functionality. Her abilities to take a total mess of a system and redesign it to make it flow professionally has taken Defender Publishing and SkyWatch TV to a whole new level of efficiency.

God's shaping wheels were spinning when he formed Joe, the little character; when He formed Allie, the ultimate organizer; when he formed Donna, the preacher-by-the-pen. Absolutely every little detail of our ministries was being formed in the womb of heaven alongside these individuals, and SkyWatch TV and Defender Publishing would not be what they are today without them.

Oh…but before I forget…

How do Nita's talents fit into all of this?

From the moment Nita was born, *way* before she met the boy from El Mirage, she had a love for the sophisticated and refined equine creatures of the field. She has never been able to fully explain why, but from her earliest memories, she was always fantasizing about horses. Horses are not typically related to ministerial endeavors, but Nita kept believing that one day she would find a way to relate the two. Throughout her life she owned several, but the timing was never right for her to keep and nurture them correctly. Horse after horse, she ended up rehoming them and feeling discouraged.

When we arrived in Missouri, we finally had the land Nita needed to invest in these animals, even as just a hobby, if not for a ministry. I bought her two full-sized horses, and she was as excited as I have ever seen her. After our very first ride together—when my belligerent, stubborn, and uncooperative horse started rolling around on the ground with me in the saddle—Nita was understandably heartbroken when the horse was deemed a threat and had to be sold. The lady who bought her had a couple of her own she was looking to sell, so Nita prepared herself for another round. However, after her visit to the lady's barn to check out what had been advertised as a "sweet gentleman of a horse" for sale, Nita landed on her back following a serious bucking tirade and was holed up in the living room recovering for a couple weeks. She wasn't giving up, though. Before her body even completely healed from the accident, she started looking for another horse. "Old Man," as we had named him, was the next to join our land. Nita's celebratory enthusiasm was short lived after Old Man sliced his chest open on the barbed-wire fence, and subsequently kicked her hard on the leg after she had been tending to his wound.

Three major close calls in such a short time—followed by years of observing that it was simply "never the right time"—led Nita to believe that this heart's desire for a horse she had felt from childhood couldn't possibly be something that God was inspiring. In her own words:

Later, I was lying on my couch, my body in pain all over, feeling like a little whipped puppy dog. It had only been a short time since I had brought these animals back into my life when Tom had been thrown, I had been bucked off, and now I had been kicked.

How could this be happening?! Why was this happening?!

For a while I remained still, wrestling with my thoughts, considering the evidence I had been given.... How were these other horse owners doing it? How did all these other lucky people have farms and ranches full of these creatures and live to see the day they could simply be enjoyed and not feared? Was I the problem? Or was I just bringing home the wrong animals? If it was meant for me to see my dreams come to fruition, what was I doing wrong? And if it wasn't meant to be, why on earth was I still pining for the day I would get to experience that joy?

Would it be too much to ask the horsie world to throw me a bone, and spare me from another lemon? (Nita Horn, *No Fences*, 163)

But, it was also during this time when Nita purchased our first miniature horse, Little Mama. She bought this animal more or less as a pet for the grandkids to dress up and play with, but the horse became so much more than that over time. It was then that Nita realized the Lord had ways of meeting the desires of our hearts, but not always how we picture it to be:

So there, that day, alone in my living room, amongst a pile of horse-wound heating pads, ice packs, and chiropractor bills, and with every muscle and joint throbbing like an old, old woman, I finally did the unthinkable.

I gave up.

I felt tears swell up in my eyes and said, "Lord, I'm way too young to feel this old. This isn't what I've dreamed of my whole life, and I'm done. Every time I try to make the desires of my heart come to pass, I am met with a resistance that I can no longer ignore. I have to simply believe that even if this horse thing was to be my will, it is clearly not yours. To that end, I will be obedient."

And with that, I felt the equine dream had been short lived, but I began making plans to re-home every horse I owned…

Except for Little Mama. She could stay.

Little Mama was harmless.

But…if Little Mama is safe, I wondered…

I can't say that it came as a sudden epiphany. It was more of a slow and gradual transition, but I started revisiting the driving motives behind my fantasies. I began to look back on all those moments in life when I felt drawn to these animals, and really reflect on what it was that I wanted all those years. Of course there was the adventure, the riding off into the sunset, the romance, the thrill of it all… But above and beyond that, there was a companionship. I never needed to impress a horse with fancy words, and that had never been my skill. These horses were always unassuming and connected with me in ways humans never could. Sure, some people find that same connection with a canine, but the horse had always been at the center of my wiring for as long as I can remember.

Was it possible, then, that the dream was right, but the concept was wrong?...

Was my lifelong dream of galloping off into the wild blue with a full-size horse and half a dozen family members merely a skewed concept? Had I...been focused so long on what I thought the package would look like that my vision was blurred to what the dream was actually leading me to?...

The lesson...helped me to revise my concepts. Remember to have an open mind when you dream. The package containing your dream may arrive on your doorstep earlier or later than you thought it was due, and it might look different than the one you thought you ordered. (Ibid., 163–166; 168; 170)

Nita no more expected this little darling of a horse to become a ministry than anything. For her, horses were incredibly fun, and we can learn as much from them as they can from us, but the notion that an entire ministry enterprise could be built around them is not a common one. God, however, had other plans. Nita relates the moment this new perception of ministry dawned on her:

...Jenny, one of my closest friends today, fell upon hard times with her father. She had to sell almost everything she had, uproot her life, and care for him during sickness. Ellie was Jenny's prized miniature horse. She had been house-trained to walk into crowded buildings and visit with people in person as a therapy horse. It appeared as if there was nothing this horse couldn't do. To some minis...a trailer was a huge mouth, a great threat. But Ellie could take an elevator to the top floor of a hospital, walk down narrow hallways, and press her nose into the hands of the injured, the ill, and the disabled, without a hint of fear.

Before Ellie, I had never even considered using a horse for this purpose. At best, my idea of reaching people for the lost through a horse might have been to let them ride while we visited, which not only paved the way for a very limited ministry endeavor, but it was also exclusive of the very people Ellie was reaching on a daily basis.

When Jenny told me she had to sell Ellie in order to care for her father, I didn't hesitate to buy her. And in owning Ellie, God opened my eyes to a whole world of possibilities, ways to love people and reach them for His Kingdom. A thought that I hadn't fathomed prior....

Something—or rather, Someone—was trying to tell me something, and I was bound to be receptive. Having just learned the lesson of being the listener instead of the speaker, I watched from a distance, and waited to hear from that small, profound voice that whispered to me in the stillness of the barn.

Ellie was...a nurturer, loved people, loved to be touched, and thrived in an atmosphere where loneliness dominated as a tool for therapy and companionship. Ellie could touch peoples' hearts when and where they needed it, in ways humanity would not. Ellie was the dawning of a new day. Ellie was a ministry...

I heard the Lord's words.

Nita, if I can bring a miniature horse out of her debilitating and internal confinement, I can do the same for you. I am not through with you yet. You have a ministry ahead of you. A personal one. One you don't even realize you've been praying for all your life. Put yourself out there. I am the Potter. You are My clay.

I'm molding you. I'm making you. And I will not place into My vessels more than they can carry, for I am the Master Handler.

And there it was.

The Creator of the universe had a plan for me. (Ibid., 203–204; 206–207)

This is only a small part of the story of how Defender Publishing and SkyWatch TV expanded to include Whispering Ponies Ranch Retreat Center—our 280-acre therapy retreat facility, as well as a premier training location that specializes in using and gifting therapy animals. Some of our greatest hopes for reaching the lost, as well as touching those who are hurting, lies within Whispering Ponies Ranch (WPR).

One of the groups we facilitated at Camp Davidson was a ministry called the Royal Family Kids Camp (RFKC). Young children who are taken from their homes and placed as a ward of the state into foster care system are sent to a campground where they are assigned to a personal counselor for one week. During this week, they are led from one activity to another while the abuse or harsh domestic conditions of their past is addressed and nurtured through trust exercises. The goal is not an attempt to repair all of the damage done in their early years, but to make a lasting and positive impact on every child present while he or she is in the midst of adults who truly care about their future.

This ministry was launched in 1990, thirty-six years ago at this time. The first and second generation of children whose lives were forever altered by that one important week have now grown. From them, *scores* of testimonies have surfaced that tell the story of how they connected with one person—just *one* person—when and where it counted, with God's incredible timing, and they later dedicated their lives to the Lord as a result. Many of these children, now men and women, have joined the RFKC staff as personal counselors, now connecting with today's generation of mistreated and hurting adolescents in ways many other adults cannot, and it is coming around full-circle.

When Nita and I began construction on our Whispering Ponies Ranch Retreat Center, we made the RFKC one of our first contacts for potential outreach. As another unbelievable twist that surfaced from our days at Camp Davidson, we discovered that the RFKC president and national director was Chris Carmichael, the son of William Carmichael—a fellow Camp and Conference Ministries board member whom I served alongside, and one of my closest personal acquaintances while we worked there. Immediately Chris agreed to fly out and meet with our WPR crew to discuss the possibilities of a ministerial partnership. With him, he brought the RFKC founder, Wayne Tesch. We discussed the numerous ways in which our mutual vision can be incorporated at WPR and how our ministry supporters such as those who *Sponsor a Pony* (see http://skywatchtv.com/sponsor-therapy-pony/) are helping this dream spread across the United States and around the world in fulfillment of James 1:27, which describes "Pure religion and undefiled before God and the Father" as ministering to orphans and widows.

We are now constructing a retreat facility to host the RFKC and ministries like theirs *at no cost to them* starting in 2017. Buildings are being raised as we speak, an RV park for volunteers is nearly done, ponds for fishing have been dug and stocked, trails are being cut in, and horses are presently under training especially for use with children. And, through the training *we*, as a family unit, received during our days at Camp Davidson, there is not a single department in this kind of ministry we cannot supervise when we are not operating the television station.

As this book has so far shown, God is alive and well in every life. He is able to take a complete nobody from El Mirage and form from them entire enterprises of ministry reaching *millions*. Not one thing that has happened in my lifetime for His purposes came independently from His design and will.

At the start of this book, I referenced the following quote:

> I have no idea how I wound up where I am. In fact, sometimes I feel like the most unqualified man on earth to be out here addressing global audiences through syndicated media on television…speaking at these huge conferences where thousands of people have crowded into large auditoriums to hear me, of all people… (Thomas Horn, in the introductory scene of Sky-Watch TV's documentary INHUMAN: The Next and Final Phase of Man Is Here, 2015)

And yet, I know *exactly* how I wound up where I am. It blows my mind to think of all God has done with the little boy from El Mirage, but there is no doubt it was all Him. I still feel like the most unqualified man on earth to be addressing such enormous audiences through the media, but I am well aware that the Creator of the universe uses the most unqualified people by our finite standards for His Kingdom. It was never about me. And from what I'm seeing lately, it may have far more to do with what God is doing in the lives of my children, the next generation, than myself.

Yet, even so, it will never be about *them*, either.

We are vessels, and from within we carry the redeeming message of Jesus Christ, which is waiting to tip and pour over the world the day we open our mouths in obedience.

Maybe your story will be like that of David, an ancient hero who slew a giant and freed all of Israel from the threat of its foes and whose life will never stop being celebrated and studied. Maybe your story began like Mary Magdalene's, but will end in a tale of the most powerful redemption leading billions to Christ. Maybe your story is that of Shiphrah or Puah or that vital seagull, whose contributions to the Kingdom of God never reach fame, but whose tiniest decisions will forever alter the lives within that sea of unnumbered people you never knew you were reaching.

Rest in knowing that no matter how your story reads, your footprint—though it may not be at the front of the line—is leading someone else behind you. You are not a mistake. You are a living, breathing child of God, fearfully and wonderfully made (Psalm 139:14).

For we are his workmanship, created in Christ Jesus for good works, which God prepared beforehand, that we should walk in them.

EPHESIANS 2:10